THE POWER OF AUTHENTICITY

THE POWER OF AUTHENTICITY

Three Principles of Leadership Success

RAJA AL GURG

Medina Publishing

First published in 2023 by Medina Publishing Ltd

50 High Street
Cowes
Isle of Wight
PO31 7RR

www.medinapublishing.com

Copyright © Raja Al Gurg, 2023

Printed and bound in the UAE by Oriental Press

ISBN Softback - 978-1-911487-75-3

ISBN eBook - 978-1-911487-76-0

Raja Al Gurg asserts her moral right to be identified as the author of this book.

CIP data: A catalogue record for this book is available at the British Library.

CONTENTS

It is only fitting that this book be dedicated to all the talented people I have worked with at the Easa Saleh Al Gurg Group, for without them I could not have achieved what I have.

I would also like to thank the diligent and caring individuals at the various industry associations and charitable organisations I have been involved with. I have learned so much from you all.

Finally, my deepest gratitude is owed to my father, the Chairman, who generously shared his leadership philosophy and taught me everything I know. He will forever inspire me.

Foreword

What is leadership? Pose this question to anyone in business and they will most likely give you an answer that centres around the word 'influence'. Leaders influence the people who follow them to fulfil their often-ambitious visions for the organisations that they lead. That is, however, where the complexity begins. As chairman of Emirates Airlines since 1985, with a current roll call of in excess of 75,000 employees who help passengers fly to more than 150 international destinations through a fleet of more than 250 aircraft, it could be said that the word 'influence' is doing some hard work here. Indeed, anyone who leads a company of any size, let alone a business on the scale of Emirates Airlines, or other organisations I chair such as Alliance Insurance Companies and Dubai Airports, will tell you that the process of influence is no simple task.

I was curious when I heard that Dr Raja Al Gurg was writing a book on leadership. She has been at the helm at the Easa Saleh Al Gurg Group for some years, meaning she too is leading a business of considerable size. In her case, the corporation she leads is a significant conglomerate which has had a huge impact on the UAE and beyond. During this time, she has earned a reputation as a determined but fair leader who has been a force for good in her business and in the many philanthropic causes she supports. It was through these latter endeavours that I had the opportunity to get to know her a little better. I was appointed Chairman of the Board of Trustees of the Al Jalila Foundation, of which Dr Raja is a member, as well as acting as Chairperson of the Board of Directors. She has played a leading role in realising the vision of HH Sheikh Mohammed bin Rashid Al Maktoum, to create an AED 300 million facility in Dubai's Healthcare City. The idea was first raised in 2012 and, in a short space of time, the Al Jalila Foundation has not only become a reality, but is now also making a significant impact on the global stage with its innovative and impactful medical research. I have attended several fund-raising galas with Dr Raja, who has been relentless in her efforts, with each event raising record-breaking donations. I have also witnessed her unwavering commitment to establishing the UAE's first cancer charity hospital. Sheikh Hamdan's hospital will be fully funded by charitable donations raised through the Al Jalila Foundation and will, I am sure, fulfil its goal of making a great impact on humanity. At the time of writing, it has already passed the halfway mark in its fundraising drive towards raising AED 750 million. This speaks volumes for the tenacity of Dr Raja's leadership and her 'nothing is impossible' attitude.

We were both attending the graduation of the Class of 22, from the Mohammed bin Rashid University of Medicine and Health Sciences (MBRU), when Dr Raja first mentioned this book. The ceremony celebrated the first cohort of 11 medical students with scholarships from Al Jalila Foundation. I was there in my role as Chancellor of MBRU and Chairman of Dubai Academic Health Corporation Board of Directors, and Dr Raja in her capacity as a board member of MBRU, as well representing Al Jalila. I was immediately intrigued. I had no doubts that Dr Raja had much to share on leadership, but how would she address such a complex subject, I asked? Having read this book, I can see that the answer to this question is, perhaps unsurprisingly, tied closely with Dr Raja's personal style of leadership. She simplifies the complexities of leading a large workforce, spread across several diverse divisions, by putting her people-first values at the core of everything she does. Her description of authentic leadership through mind, heart and soul is built upon the firm foundation of her own strong values. People follow leaders who value what they value and, in doing so, will readily accept their influence and work hard to fulfil their vision. The opposite is also true: we reject leaders who show values that do not align with our own, and will therefore not allow ourselves to be influenced in the way they wish. This is the basis for positive influence and strong leadership.

One of the themes of this book is that the growth and success of the Easa Saleh Al Gurg Group has, in many ways, mirrored that of the UAE and I would agree with the connection being made. We are at a very exciting time in the history of our region, with much investment here and abroad. Thanks to a carefully laid out strategy, we are seeing rapid expansion in a multitude of sectors, from my own specialism, air transport, to tourism, industry and technology, to name just a few categories of business which will define our future. We are also enjoying a substantial rise in entrepreneurship which in turn has expanded the private sector. For this intense period of advancement to be a continued success, we need more good leaders to guide us through the challenges all businesses will face along the way. We will also need for their teams to be inspired and to follow. This will further fuel our already diversified economy, creating the jobs and opportunities that will underpin our ambitious plans to be a global epicentre of business. We are not in a unique situation though. Organisations the world over need a good supply of exceptional, inspirational leaders, particularly at a time of generally sluggish growth, as we have seen following the pandemic.

As Dr Raja wisely points out at the start of this book, no two leaders are the same. However, there is much that can be learned from this particular business leader and her authentic style of leadership. Strong values are vital for the next generation of leaders as they seek to influence the culture and climate of their workforces. Setting and adhering to the values they identify will underpin and guide decision-making. It will also afford them greater clarity around who they are and the vision they are working towards.

All business leaders seek to raise the bar when it comes to innovation and growth. However, they will only achieve their goals through the efforts of their teams, by motivating them to be better, go faster, reach higher. To do this, people need to be inspired by the vision and the values that underpin that vision. Authentic leadership is powerful leadership. It is the key to harnessing the power of a team and, of course, influence.

His Highness Sheikh Ahmed bin Saeed Al Maktoum

President of the Dubai Civil Aviation Authority, Chairman of Dubai Airports, Chairman and Chief Executive of the Emirates Airline and Group

Introduction
Characteristics of a Leader

*What do people think of you
when you leave the room?*

When I took over as managing director of the Easa Saleh Al Gurg Group, there were few Emirati women in prominent roles in business, let alone heading up a conglomerate like this one.

Growing up in Dubai in the 1960s and 1970s, I witnessed a small coastal town of no more than 30,000 develop into the globally recognised metropolis and tourist destination it is today. Alongside these remarkable changes was a steady increase in women's participation in business and public life. My generation saw a marked increase in women receiving higher education and entering the workforce, balancing the responsibilities of motherhood with full-time jobs.

My late father, Sir Easa Saleh Al Gurg, established the Easa Saleh Al Gurg Group in 1960, at the onset of the rapid transformation of our region that would ensue in the proceeding decades. The Group's first office building was set in the neighbourhood in which I grew up, Bur Dubai, overlooking the traditional dhows and bustling maritime trade of Dubai Creek, which then cut through the middle of the town. In 1971,

1

when Dubai joined six other neighbouring emirates to form the United Arab Emirates, the Easa Saleh Al Gurg Group was just launching its early operations in real estate, while also extending its business to work alongside partners from Europe to North America. As Dubai transformed from a regional centre of trade to an international business hub, the Group extended its business into a wide range of operations, covering everything from retail to consumer goods to manufacturing. The Group now encompasses 27 companies within its portfolio and has partners with many renowned international businesses. In essence, the Group embodied the ingenuity and entrepreneurial spirit that has defined the UAE since its inception.

When I was appointed managing director of the Group, it was amidst these extraordinary changes. It also coincided with a concerted move to elevate more women into leadership roles in our region, fulfilling the vision of Sheikh Zayed, the founding father and driving force behind the formation of the UAE.

The message of empowering women in leadership roles was one I could get behind. As a mother, I was acutely aware of the influence my own new leadership position would have on those around me and my community. I appreciated the respect needed to be in such a position and approached it as such.

Despite working long hours learning to be an effective leader in my new position, and having little experience of public speaking, I agreed to almost every request to attend events and spread the message about the power of women leaders in the UAE. It gave me immense pleasure to see how rapidly women in the UAE were growing in confidence in response to our campaign, finding top positions in everything from academia to technology. Whenever I gave talks in the UAE, I would stay behind for as long as I could, answering question after question. *How do I get started?* I was asked. *What sector would you recommend? Where do I find the best team?* I was fairly certain that, when I ventured further afield, the wider world would be just as curious, if not more so, to hear what I had to say. Surely our ambitious plans were something the whole world wanted to get behind? After all, it is to everyone's benefit to grow the pool of exceptional leaders, and there were so many women just waiting to be given the chance. This is perhaps why I was taken aback by some feedback from one of my first international speeches.

The talk was at a conference run by a professional services firm. My speech seemed to have been received quite well and I had rather enjoyed it. I'd practised it over and over in front of my children at home. They'd perched on the end of my bed, like a row of cats, listening intently. When they felt I had got it right, they said, 'That's it, Mama, you've got it now. Stop!' Fortunately, my audience at this professional services conference were less abrupt.

I spent the rest of the day at the event, listening to the other speeches and speaking with some of the delegates, who had come from all over the world. Just as I was about to leave, the organiser of the conference came hurrying over. When I had met her on my arrival the previous day, she had been cool and assured, but now she looked breathless and flustered.

'Mrs Raja, are you leaving?' she asked.

I nodded and smiled, wondering what the problem might be.

'I have to get something off my chest,' she said.

'Please, do that.' I smiled encouragingly.

The woman paused, clearly unsure whether to carry on.

'I don't want you to think badly of me,' she said at last.

'I won't think badly of you.'

She was silent again, before taking a deep breath.

'When we were choosing the speakers and they put your name forward, I told them that I felt you were going to be difficult to deal with. It would all just be too complicated...' Her voice trailed off.

'And did you find me "difficult"?' I asked.

The woman broke into a smile for the first time since we'd met again that evening.

3

'No. When you arrived, you came out and mingled with everyone. There was absolutely no difference between you and us.'

'Well, that is how I am.'

'Yes, I know that now. And I regret saying that about you.'

I appreciated this woman's honesty in correcting her mistake. She is not the only person to carry preconceptions about leadership in the Middle East, or more specifically about women in top roles. They see the hijab and find it hard to get beyond that. Aside from the irony that thanks to COVID we've all had to get used to wearing face coverings in recent years, regardless of our religion, this does seem a rather naive way of assessing a person. How I dress has nothing whatsoever to do with the quality of my leadership or my business achievements. When I look at other people, I don't form an opinion about them from their way of dressing. I see them as a person and talk to them because they are a human being, just like me. They may have been brought up in a different environment, but I view that as a positive thing, knowing it will make for an interesting and enriching conversation.

Things have got a little better in the intervening 20 years, between the time I gave that speech and now, but people like me still don't fit into the expectations of those in the Western world. Even now, when women say they are going to take up a position in the UAE, the response is often one of feigned horror.

'Are women allowed to work?'

This is the cue for me to patiently explain that women are not just *allowed* to work in the UAE, but the country has encouraged female workers since its inception. The UAE has led the way with women's empowerment in the Gulf region, with women making up 59 per cent of the UAE labour force. There is even a law that makes it mandatory to appoint a woman to the board of every company and government agency. The government's Gender Balance Council, which was set up to ensure women have equal opportunities and representation in the public sector, has helped see women make up 66 per cent of the public sector workforce, 35 per cent of the health sector and 20 per cent of the social affairs sector. The government are 'walking the walk' too, by appointing women to nearly a third of its cabinet posts. In 2018, it became enshrined in law that women get equal salaries and opportunities. So yes, women *can*, and *do*, work.

And yet the stereotypes persist. Sometimes the only way to deflect them is to deal with the comments with humour. One of the questions that always amuses me is when I'm asked if we are all still living in tents, moving around on camels.

'No, we leave the tents for the tourists,' I say with a smile. 'It seems some of those visiting on holiday like sleeping in them in the baking hot sun, and riding on camels.'

I have made it my mission to change perceptions about doing business in my region and, of course, have maintained my role supporting women. I have spent a lot of time thinking about these misconceptions about the UAE and, in particular, the view of women in leadership roles. I've moved past the notion that the outside world doesn't want to hear, or indeed believe, that we are more advanced than the outdated view that prevails. Instead, I have chosen to address the issue more broadly, weighing what I have seen and heard against the fact that women the world over face barriers to achieving top positions. As my conversation at the professional services conference revealed, there is still a large degree of unconscious bias (from women as well as men, surprisingly). While much is now made of inclusivity, diversity and equity, there is still a deeply entrenched view that all leaders should somehow look, behave and perform in exactly the same way. Or, more accurately, there is just one 'good' way to lead.

I am still frequently asked about the differences between male and female leadership. This is usually alongside pointed questions about how I balance family and work, or, if I had to choose between the two, which would it be? To me, this is entirely the wrong question. I would never sacrifice my family life and have never had to. Nor do I believe I need to lead 'like a man'. I have always shied away from emphasising just one kind of leadership. Leadership has to come from within. You have to know how to lead yourself before you try to lead anyone else, and this very much depends on the type of person you are. We all think and act differently, and we should celebrate those differences. All leaders, male and female, from the UAE and beyond, are individuals. We have our strengths and, yes, some weaknesses. We use them to lead in our own way, and the proof of the success of our endeavours is in how our companies grow and flourish. It's in how we develop the next generation of leaders and the legacy that we leave behind.

My reason for writing this book is to share my version of leadership and what I have learned over more than four decades in this position. It may not be your version of leadership, but there may be parts of it that resonate and which you find useful. A leader is, after all, made from a combination of their knowledge and previous experiences, and I am here to share mine. Our effectiveness as leaders depends on how we discover those skills and then use them. As leaders, we can't live in isolation. We can learn a lot from how other people face their challenges.

Much of what I have learned about leadership has been shaped under the wise tutelage of my father. As many of the lessons he taught me were in a professional setting, I will often refer to him in this book as the Chairman, drawing a clear boundary between his role as my father and his former status as the head of the company.

Other lessons I have learned elsewhere. The most obvious resource is my own leadership of the companies in our conglomerate. When I was appointed managing director of the Easa Saleh Al Gurg Group, I didn't simply become a leader because I had a grand title. You become a leader when you go through experiences, both of success and failure. Failure leads to success, because when something doesn't work, you try to do it in a different way. If that doesn't work, you will try another way still. One day, it will click, and you will achieve what you set out to do. This is why I'd rather not be called a leader. I prefer the term 'achiever'! Or perhaps I don't need a label at all.

One of the other important lessons I have learned is to be humble. Showing off doesn't get you respect. In fact, it elicits quite the opposite effect. I would prefer my leadership and achievements to speak for themselves.

Equally powerful is what I have learned from my family. When you have a family, it teaches patience. Before I had children, I had a bad habit of rushing into decisions, because I always believed it was better to get things done and out of the way. When my children were small, I realised that decisions are much better made when you've had time to calm down. It is much more important to take the emotion out of judgement, and there is rarely a need to rush into anything.

It was one of my sons who taught me this lesson. He was always full of mischief and could never sit still for long. We had a routine where the children were all collected from school at 1:30pm and, after lunch, I would sit with them while they did their homework, acting as both mother and teacher. To guarantee that they would attend to their studies, I would put an alarm clock on the table between us.

'Do not move until this alarm goes off,' I would say. 'Once it does, you can go and play. However, if you move before that…'

I would then pretend to read my newspaper while they scribbled away at their textbooks.

One day, I was in my usual seat, staring at my newspaper, when I became aware that my son had reached forward and switched off the alarm clock. I watched as he crossed the room, picked up a pencil sharpener and twisted his pencil in the hole. When he was finished, he held the pencil up to the light that poured in through the window, nodded in satisfaction at its sharpness and returned to his seat at the table. As he sat down, he reached across and deftly flicked the alarm clock back on.

'I saw what you did,' I said, folding my newspaper and putting it down.

'Yes, I stopped the clock,' he said. 'It was because of the timing. You said I had to finish my homework within the time, and I needed to sharpen my pencil. I had to stop the clock, or I wouldn't have had time.'

He was right. He taught me that one should stop the clock now and again.

I have also learned much from my own culture. Despite the misconceptions, Arabs are like people all over the world. We're down to earth and, most of all, we truly value and respect the people who are around us. The people who work for me and with me are crucial to the success of my business.

I spend a lot of time with my team and, when I meet them, I am always natural with them and don't only speak to give them instructions. I like to joke with them and relax. I want them to be happy. This is my philosophy. I think it is a good test for a leader to imagine what their people would say about them when they are not in the room.

How then, would I summarise my style of leadership? Perhaps I should start by saying what it is not. Many leaders focus their attention on the external world, concerning themselves with results, structure, technology and processes. It is my view that these things are simply a manifestation of our internal worlds. It is our internal world and how we influence change that make the difference in leadership. Once you see the results in the external world, it is already too late to change them. Our internal world is led by our mind, heart and soul. The mind describes our *mental energy*. My entire career has been marked by a thirst to learn more, become wiser and more knowledgeable, and therefore a better leader. The heart is just as important for a leader. This is our *emotional energy*.

It is how we drive a sense of belonging in our organisations, and how we help our people not just understand our values and culture but feel actively invested in it. Finally, there is our soul, or *spiritual energy*. This is what comes from knowing who you are, why you are here and that you are doing something bigger than yourself. It is also the legacy you leave behind, which is something that is at the heart of a family business like mine. Get the balance between all three of these leadership characteristics right and you will be a truly authentic leader.

I have divided this book into three parts, to describe each of these three characteristics in more detail, with the first part focusing on the mind, the second on the heart and the final part addressing the soul. In each section, I have expanded upon what I believe to be the key elements of leadership, which, when taken together, combine into a powerful force of authentic leadership. I have illustrated them with stories of my time as a leader. Some of this content might not fit into the ubiquitous one-size-fits-all notion of what a leader should be. In fact, I hope it does not. I have something to share that I believe is far stronger and more powerful. If it changes your perception of the UAE, and of women leaders in particular, so much the better. Let me take you on a journey to show you the true power of authentic leadership and the value of thinking a little differently.

Raja Al Gurg, February 2023

MIND

Intellectual Energy

So much of leadership begins in the mind. What does leading with our minds really mean, though? It is where we manage our thoughts, so we can respond to circumstances in a more measured way, rather than being pulled in one direction or another by circumstance and falling victim to a pattern of quick, emotional, knee-jerk responses that might not be appropriate to the situation. By actively taking efforts to be more mentally agile and to properly weigh up the available facts we become better able to make rational, effective decisions. None of this is to say that the occasional quick decision is a bad thing. They are often an essential part of leadership, particularly in highly pressurised situations. However, if there is a foundation of solid knowledge across all the decisions you make, fast or slow, the outcome will always be better.

Leaders who rely on their intellect tend to be more focused and goal orientated. It's a process that helps prioritise the bigger picture and think in the long term. By welcoming the opportunity to study and develop ourselves as we strive for success and improvement, we are more likely to champion new projects. When we get involved in a project, we look to get results and relish the opportunity to overcome challenges.

Leaders who are keen to develop their mind-power tend to encourage the people around them to behave in the same way. I always want my team to share my thirst for self-development because I know it will develop a more independent workforce, where everyone feels empowered to think for themselves. When something doesn't go as expected, their first instinct is to try to find a solution rather than expecting someone else to fix their problems. When people on a team learn to use their mind effectively, they are more willing to evaluate past decisions and experiences to see what can be learned for the future. Once we are able to explore and think more seriously about how we manage our work, we will become more effective.

1

The Six Main Functions of Leadership

Leadership is a business of all.
Know how important you are.

The broadest definition of leadership is the accomplishment of a goal through the assistance of others. This brief description doesn't do justice to the many and varied skills required to achieve this. It certainly doesn't get close to identifying the qualities required for authentic leadership, from the long-term development of the team, to motivating individuals to work towards a shared vision, to protecting the values that underpin the organisation.

As per the title of this chapter, a leader is crucial in this endeavour, playing a central role in every aspect of the business. But an authentic leader does not achieve success by flexing their power or commanding their team to follow. They create an environment where everyone around them can be at their most effective. This can occur in many ways, but to break it down I have divided the 'business of all' into six main functions of leadership.

1. Policy making and planning

One of the most essential elements of the leadership role is to create a structured plan for the business going forward. While leaders generally start out with good intentions, this planning process is often restricted to corporate objectives and budgets that are then cascaded down into various business divisions. The primary focus is on the profits generated each year by each division, usually calculated in relation to the required percentage improvement over the previous year's performance. These annual strategies will almost always take into account major changes to the market. From our own positioning, for example, there have been many changes to government regulations and tax policies in the UAE as it pursues its ambitions to take up more of a position at the centre of world trade. In previous years, we built a very successful business working as licensees for international brands which were not allowed to operate independently in our region. That rule changed in 2021, when new laws were introduced to allow foreign investors to own up to 100 per cent of local companies, allowing international brands to trade in Dubai independently. While many of our brand partners have indicated they are very keen to continue to trade with us, we need to be sure that every aspect of our business is in tune with these changes and that we are well-positioned going forward. The same goes for recent moves to extend the tax regime in the UAE, which required us to change some policies in the business. Meanwhile, on a global scale, there are constant supply chain issues to consider, as well as changes to the economic landscape, all of which have an impact.

In our business, as with any other, there are many less visible aspects to corporate operations that also need to be attended to. These elements may not seem hugely significant on a day-to-day basis, certainly compared to overall profit forecasts or shifts in government strategy, but left ignored, they can undermine these bold targets on a significant basis.

Very often, businesses continue doing things in a certain way because they have always been done that way. After all, 'if it ain't broke, don't fix it', as the saying goes. However, a review of some of these long-standing practices and policies that are part of the daily operation of the business will produce some surprises. Market dynamics change all the time, and there may well be some more cost-effective options which will vastly improve the day-to-day operation of the business, whether it is introducing improved technology or simply streamlining age-old practices.

We have initiated a regular in-depth review process across all 27 of our companies. It is an intense exercise, running over several months. Representatives from each division are charged with reviewing all the legal changes that have had an impact on their part of the business over an agreed period. Some of these changes may be minor and may only slightly impact the division, but some can have considerable implications for the whole business. The general managers of each division will then review policies in each of their departments, from HR to Finance, taking in every element from how client payments are made and approved to cash advances paid to staff on an emergency basis. Each historic policy is examined to see if we are following the most efficient strategy for the organisation we are today.

During the period of the company-wide review, which spans several months, there will be committee meetings every two weeks where everyone who is involved in the review gets together to update their colleagues on progress. Often, the changes reported by one division will be pertinent to other parts of the business, triggering new discussions to explore whether they can be implemented elsewhere. Once the review process is complete, progress continues to be monitored, so any necessary changes can be swiftly introduced. Otherwise, the entire planning strategy is re-started two years after the close of the previous one.

The benefit of scheduling these regular company-wide reviews means long- and short-term opportunities are on the radar and the whole team is always focused on the future vision for the business. Corporate objectives and financial targets are still crucial, but this process feeds into them and protects the bottom line by improving the efficiency of each unit while working to future-proof the company.

2. Setting goals

When there are no clear goals, a business will always suffer. Every project is entirely different from the last, so there can't be a one-size-fits-all goal for everything. Besides, some projects last for a couple of days, while others stretch over months. A wise leader takes a step back and puts their mind to what they want their organisation to achieve with each new task, as well as how it will be achieved and by when. The right team then needs to be chosen to fulfil the brief and the goals effectively relayed to them, broken down according to who is charged with fulfilling each task. Working towards clearly set goals is motivating and, in turn, improves performance.

There are a number of challenges that every leader must face when setting goals. The first is how ambitious to make them. Hard goals can be more motivating than easy ones, because when they are achieved, it feels like more of an accomplishment. However, there is a balance. Teams need to be stretched but not overwhelmed. Likewise, there is a balance to be found in the number of goals shared with a team. If a team is faced with multiple goals that all contribute to a main project, they will become concerned about whether they will be able to fulfil them all, which can be demotivating. They may switch the focus of their efforts to the ones that are easier to achieve so they at least can be seen to be making some progress. Unfortunately, the goals they prioritise might not necessarily be the ones that are going to add the most value to the business.

There is also the question of how rigid the goals are. A leader will have a clear vision of what they want to achieve when they set targets, but they must ask themselves how prescriptive they are about how the team will get from A to B. If they are too authoritative in their instructions, they run the risk of stifling innovation and new ideas. Growth comes from being flexible, adaptable and open to different ways of realising goals. Plus, when there is an opportunity for the team to contribute, they become more engaged.

One of the most important moments in goal setting is when the plan is briefed to the team. This is the time when something that began as a great idea, supported by research, is put into action. It's one of my favourite parts of the process and the most important step in making sure a strategy is successfully pursued. Here, a leader will spend time with their team, talking to them about the project in general and what it will take to achieve the agreed target. The objective is to sell the idea, so everyone becomes enthusiastic about it. Thus, it's helpful to begin with a broad overview, backed with key figures to show why it is so important. It is a lot easier to sell an idea when it is backed with data to show its viability. To encourage buy-in, discussion and debate should be encouraged, so that everyone feels they've had a creative role in the process and immediately become more invested in the outcome. No goal, or indeed solution, comes without some negatives. It is important to be upfront about them, so that everyone can properly prepare and there are no surprises down the road.

3. Coordination and liaison between teams

The leadership role extends far beyond simply setting goals for individual projects. It is our role to be constantly forward-looking, creating a vision for the future. But we don't create that vision alone.

We do it alongside our teams by constantly asking them, What is new? What is next? What can we do better? Once we agree on that vision, we share it with the whole team, aligning the interests of all of the various individuals. In our case, this means ensuring that those in each business division coordinate with each other, and also across all of the divisions, towards achieving our common goal.

This might seem easy when you see it written here in black and white, but it isn't. There will always be some people who don't buy into the vision, or don't like the idea of making any changes. Even those who understand the vision can get distracted because their departments have their own objectives to meet. The big question is how does a leader take *everyone* with them and surround them all with positive energy, so they can work together towards the overall vision?

Coordination and liaison between teams is the key to helping various groups work together and strive for a common goal. It's the art of getting individuals with different backgrounds, perspectives and thought processes to give their best.

As indicated here, planning for the future is essential to my organisation. However, this process is useless unless the contents of the plan are widely shared throughout the business. Everyone needs to understand the vision and the part they play in it. This means providing a clear roadmap for the whole team. As well as keeping everyone focused, to drive accountability, so individuals take responsibility for their own roles and hold each other accountable for theirs.

Communication is key to this process. With teams spread out across different locations, there needs to be a centralised hub of information that everyone can access with all the data needed to achieve the results. Likewise, there needs to be regular meetings across departments to share and exchange information.

Care needs to be taken to ensure that these meetings create meaningful outcomes. This is not a case of meetings for the sake of meetings. Getting everyone in one room can create a strange, artificial environment at the best of times. When a group of people are tasked with spending time together in a small space, with only an hour or even just half an hour to resolve an issue or agree parameters on a particular project, things can drift if left unchecked. Ideally, meetings are carefully planned, with notes shared ahead of time, outlining the objectives in a transparent, easy-to-understand manner.

One of the goals of this process is to encourage discussion between departments, or divisional leaders, so everyone gets to learn more about the progress of initiatives in other areas of the business, and any challenges they face. Everyone who attends the meeting should be given a chance to get a say, regardless of their seniority. There is no point in one division presenting its progress while everyone listens in silence. It means their actions won't be properly explored, because everyone is too quick to nod and say that will do. Again, there needs to be active steps to encourage interaction.

It is always possible to tell who is and who isn't listening, who is interested and who has zoned out. I always want to hear from the person in the room who pipes up and says it won't work and why. This is not a negative. A different point of view when respectfully communicated is always welcome, because it is an alternative way of considering a situation. This is the prompt that will get everyone in the room to think through the issue thoroughly and collaborate more effectively. A culture of open and honest discussion comes into its own here.

It is crucial to celebrate the wins with the team. When an organisation reaches a milestone, or a project is successfully completed, everyone who contributed should take a share of the credit. It cultivates trust and respect among team members from across the business. These celebrations don't need to be too elaborate. A lunch for the team works well. What is important is the activity gives team members the chance to get together and share in their success.

4. Seizing the initiative

Steady, or even better, *strong* growth is something every business leader wants to deliver. It is not something every leader can consistently achieve, though. Those leaders who want to outperform their competitors must have a different mindset. They need to think and act differently to constantly explore opportunities inside and outside the business, and then commit to fulfilling them. In short, growth-orientated leaders need to take the initiative.

Growth always begins with an ambitious plan. A leader is in charge of an $X billion organisation and they want to increase its size by 50 per cent in a given period. How do they do that? Our approach is to encourage each individual department or division to weigh up what it can do to create that sort of exponential growth and then to find ways to help make it happen.

Inspire a shared vision

Our ambitious strategy for growth is supported by the culture we've created, which encourages individuals on the team to come forward with ideas in every part of the business. This produces a regular pipeline of ideas. A pool of funds has been set aside to develop innovations and the best ideas get priority. There is a robust process to evaluate them. It begins with a feasibility study, which analyses the scope of the project, the proposed return and break-even costs. The resulting detailed report is studied by an investment committee, made up of a team of senior managers from across the business. The committee is invited to vote on each idea, which is first presented to the Group CEO and then myself for the final sign off.

I'll give you an example of just such a process.

The division in question here was a manufacturing business that was already doing quite well, which is a good starting point. After all, imagining a growth strategy for a failing business entails twice the amount of effort, requiring a programme to stem the losses *and then* implement a plan to increase business. In this case, while the manufacturer was succeeding, closer inspection of its books revealed warning signs. It was already up to its limit in production capacity, even though it had plenty of orders on the books. The general manager came forward to say that a competitor's facility was up for sale and suggested that we take it over to expand production and grow this business. The only issue was that the competitor's unit was three times the size of our existing facility. It was clear our facility needed to expand, but it would be a bold strategy indeed to do a deal like this.

We needed to move quickly, because opportunities like this don't come along often, but we also needed to thoroughly evaluate the suggestion. We were, after all, looking at tripling the size of the business. Our investment committee evaluated the pros and cons, looked at the market and assessed whether there was enough potential business for a larger unit and the appetite to buy from us. We also looked at whether an enlarged unit could be run as smoothly as the existing one. We didn't want to drive customers away because projects were delayed, or the output didn't match the quality they were used to. Consideration also needed to be given to raw materials and whether we'd be able to source enough for the increased capacity. Also, were the machines we'd inherit from the new site as good in quality as the ones we were used to?

The input of the general manager into the evaluation was invaluable. His evidence and knowledge of the market helped to convince the senior team that there was an opportunity we could seize.

Taking initiative is not simply a question of pressing the 'go' button when the data proves it is a good plan. We still need to build organisational buy-in so everyone is on board. This is where research and planning pay dividends once again. We can use them to create significant and credible targets to show how the plan will create value for the business and why it is worth investing the resources. The plan was shared with shareholders first, to get their buy-in, and once that was achieved, it was used to inspire the team who needed to implement the opportunity.

Leaders who are focused on growth fully understand the importance of pursuing and then taking initiatives. This is how to create consistent and significant growth. This may, at times, involve strategic shifts into different channels, or innovating by changing the emphasis on core products or simply by identifying pockets of untapped potential in the existing business. The common and deciding factors are clarity of vision, the willingness to take bold steps and the ability to seize the initiative.

Not every idea we receive will be taken forward like this. However, we always encourage the person who made the suggestion to develop their idea or come back with another suggestion at any time. Everyone in the organisation knows they will always get a good hearing. Ours is a business that is always ready to seize the initiative and innovate.

5. Delegation

Leaders have a key function to play in helping their team perform at the highest level. Thus, as well as assigning roles to individuals most suited to them, active steps need to be taken to help them do their jobs efficiently and productively.

It is impossible to be a good leader without delegating. Early on in anyone's leadership career they will face the challenge when transitioning from *doing* to *leading*. Everyone in this position has had the feeling that they'd be better off doing something themselves. *It will take just as long to explain it!* But, as the leadership role grows, this isn't practical. Sure, a new leader may manage to do it all at first. Perhaps they will get up earlier and work later. This is not the route to effective leadership, though. The more unnecessary work we hold onto, the more it diminishes our standing as a leader. It also signals to the team that their leader doesn't really trust them. The transition that needs to be made here is towards shaping the thoughts and ideas of others. This is what will bring the leadership priorities to life.

Say, for example, I wanted someone to lead a new project. Delegation always begins by finding the right person for the task. It is easy to choose someone who has already proved themself, but I am also keen to give people a chance. This is a good way of developing new talent and will also help engage the team. If someone steps forward and says, 'Give me an opportunity!' I am always keen to support them.

When delegating a task like this, it is best to begin by giving the context, explaining why something matters and how it fits into the broader picture. It is much better to express the reasons why it will *matter* to the business. It may, for example, lead to us operating in an unexplored sector, which this person can champion and, at the same time, learn new skills. To help them fully commit, it's helpful to clarify both the expected outcome and their role in making it happen.

Sometimes, when leaders delegate a task, it is outside the comfort zone of the individual assigned to it. It is the people who put their hand up anyhow and say, 'Let me do it,' that I watch closely. They are leadership material.

Sometimes space is better than interference

How much should a leader stay involved once a task is delegated? It very much depends on the importance of the task and its potential impact on the organisation as a whole. It is up to individual leaders to judge this. There is a balance to be had between being too involved, and potentially micromanaging, and being completely hands off and perhaps missing crucial moments where intervention may be essential. A skill all leaders must perfect is gauging what level of support or feedback individual team members require.

When a leader is proficient at empowering others to deliver their best, they free up their time. The contribution of others increases their capacity to do more.

6. Motivation

Leadership can't exist in isolation, but, when in charge of a company of significant size, how do you motivate the whole team? I have found that this can be achieved by taking your people with you. Simply telling people what to do won't engage them and won't result in exceptional performance.

My goal is to create a culture of team ownership where everyone feels fully empowered and invested in the business. The company doesn't belong to me; it belongs to us. It is in this environment of partnership that everyone will step up and take equal responsibility for the quality of their work and its outcome. When everyone feels invested in the company's future they will collaborate more, communicate better and focus on growth.

But how do you create this environment of belonging? The essence of my strategy is a theme that runs throughout this book. I listen to the team, encourage them to make decisions and put their mark on the business because I genuinely value what they have to say. In return, I am open and transparent with them. Appealing to their human qualities, I focus on team members' positive emotions, which form the basis for their motivation.

I invest a lot of time strengthening relationships with the team by meeting with them face to face and hearing their suggestions, ideas or problems. Decisions are not simply imposed on anyone. Everyone feels like they are part of the thinking process. There is another side to this too. Regularly speaking with people on a one-to-one basis is an opportunity to get to know them as individuals and to find out what motivates them. I like to know more about their interests and what it is they are passionate about, both inside and outside of work. It is for this same reason that I keep informal channels open, and it's not unusual for me to drop team members a WhatsApp message to check in on how they are doing if I have not seen them for a few days.

It is also crucial to provide resources so everyone can fulfil their potential. Earlier in this chapter, I described the process for team members to share their ideas with the investment committee. Successful ideas are given full funding and resources to go ahead, which is of course exceptionally motivating for the person concerned because it shows their input is highly valued. Equally importantly though, anyone who wishes to present an idea is given support and guidance. We provide all the facilities they need to learn meaningful new skills. Assistance is also on tap to improve the quality of their overall presentation to the committee. Our corporate finance team has, for example, devised a template, so even if the individual concerned is not confident with numbers, the process is straightforward. We also help by setting up sub-committees, which provide a platform to brainstorm and better develop ideas before they are put in front of the main committee. If the development process requires input from another department, we are always happy to facilitate it.

This same process feeds another aspect of motivation: the need for purpose. We all want to achieve something at work. Creating something meaningful improves our mood and boosts productivity. Everyone in the organisation has the opportunity to grow their side of the business and to be recognised for their innovation and forward-thinking. You cannot under-estimate how important this is for motivation.

Treat people in this way and they will open up and flourish. I have seen it happen many times. Individuals will join us and, at first, will seem nervous and unsure of themselves. Over time though, they will become more relaxed. They will realise that we want to hear what they have to say. Once they feel they can grow as a person, things will really start happening for them and for our company.

2

Running Efficient Projects

Every project is an adventure.

There are many challenges to running a significant conglomerate, not least the various aspects to our business, from buying and selling goods to managing significant projects, often many at a time. This is where the 'mind' side of leadership comes to the fore, since careful management and monitoring is required to ensure each individual element goes smoothly.

While always intense, projects do eventually come to a close, giving everyone some breathing room. In what little spare time I have, I am involved as a trustee and advisor in a few charitable endeavours. For ethical reasons, and to avoid a conflict of interest, I like to keep my charitable work entirely separate from my business interests, and I appreciate the opportunity to adopt a purely altruistic focus and make use of my project leadership skills to help establish medical or educational facilities, for example.

Project management requires a special sort of intelligent and visionary leadership, which is why I believe it is useful to look at this side of our business in more detail.

Leadership in this space requires a multitude of skills, from strategic thinking to problem solving to team building. With several projects on the go at once, each project needs to be carefully steered towards its conclusion. If this doesn't happen, there will be delays, potential conflicts between the team and even with the client, and the project may not come in on budget.

Each of our project managers plays a vital part in fulfilling the goals of every project: to deliver the best outcome for our partners and clients and grow profits for our organisation. Therefore, I encourage them all to take personal ownership of the projects they lead. The role of leadership in this context is to define the scope of the project, plan it, execute the plan and continuously monitor it.

Before we get into the detail, let me break the basics of project leadership down.

Plan and define the scope of projects

I often say that every project is like an adventure – hence the title of this chapter. There are so many elements involved, and the requirements for each are so different from the previous one. It is for this reason that every project tender must begin with a detailed plan, recording the project's precise scope and timeline. This is, without a doubt, the most important part of the process. Everyone on the project management team is encouraged to read and explore all the information about the project and the client commissioning it to create this plan. Plans are the foundation that everything else is built upon. Without them, all that follows will be chaotic, which can lead to disruption and delays.

The size of a project dictates the leadership capacity that is needed

A key part of this plan is to draw up detailed costings. It is crucial to know the full cost of every aspect of a project and the projected profit.

While accuracy is essential and a considerable number of substantial costs will most likely be involved, this should not be a complicated process, particularly when you are surrounded by the best team available. Experts can be hand-picked to work on each section, according to their personal expertise. Then all the various sections that are created can be brought together into one master document.

Allocating resources

Following on from the plan, there needs to be a clear allocation of resources, according to the size and skills of the team required. Thanks to the detailed plan, along with the due diligence around the scope of the project, the project leader will fully understand the task ahead of them and what they need to get out of their team. They can pinpoint the right individual with the best mix of skills to be responsible for each aspect of the job.

Communicating between stakeholders and teams

The bigger the project, the more communication required. Strong leadership is needed to coordinate the activities of all team members as they progress through the project plan. At the same time, the client and other stakeholders, such as statutory bodies that may be involved in the approvals process, need to be kept firmly in the loop. Processes need to be in place for a regular smooth exchange of information at all the various stages of project execution.

Reviewing milestones

Project leaders are, of course, responsible for making sure the work progresses as per the plan and should monitor each milestone according to the original project schedule.

Monitoring resources

The goal of every project is to deliver the expected outcome to the schedule within budget. Therefore, close monitoring of both elements is key. Any variation in expectation around the performance of resources at each stage can have an impact on the success, or otherwise, of a project.

Managing risk

In an ideal world, everything will proceed smoothly. But we don't live in an ideal world. Therefore, the potential risks with any project should be anticipated, mapped out and a mitigation strategy created. Before the project even begins, we go through each element of the schedule, asking ourselves: what can go wrong and, if something does, how will we deal with it? Will it be an easy problem to resolve, or will it take a considerable amount of resources? In addition, what are the cost implications? These potential issues are all meticulously logged and shared with the teams. Then, each time a project leader touches base with their team, any looming problems can be raised, so the mitigation strategies can start to be implemented where necessary.

Resolving conflict

Another troubleshooting measure is to keep on top of any potential clashes among the teams involved. Smooth team coordination is key to efficient project leadership. If there are signs of disagreements, leaders need to step in to resolve them at the earliest opportunity.

Project teams: bigger can be better

Managing multiple projects at the same time and keeping track of all the moving pieces can get complicated. It can sometimes be difficult to know what to prioritise and how to get the teams involved to effectively manage their workload. Occasionally, it is possible to descend into a situation where some project teams perform far better than others.

This was a situation we faced with one of our divisions that was working on a large project. The project in question was not going well. It had suffered from a number of delays, there was a cost over-run and the client was becoming restless. In truth, the person in charge of the team was not the right person for the job. Looking back, it was clear to see that while he was perfectly competent, his skill set had not grown in line with the size of contracts we were winning.

My senior team were gathered together to discuss the project.

'I am starting to think we may need to get rid of this company altogether,' one of the executives suggested. 'It has become a real headache.'

One of the other members of the executive team had a rather surprising suggestion in response. He put forward the idea of amalgamating it with another of our project-based businesses. While this other business was centred around different types of products, it worked in a complementary field and was hugely successful. In fact, it had been steadily growing its project business on the back of its reputation for smoothly completing projects on time and on budget.

On the face of it, the idea of creating one big division to house all our projects seemed counter-intuitive. Would the liabilities of the poorly performing company bring down the better-run division? This executive didn't believe so. He was convinced that, together, both businesses would be stronger. Planning and managing all the team's projects in one place would improve visibility across all our projects.

After giving it due thought, I gave the idea my blessing. It is never my preference to close down a division. If there is a possibility of reviving it, I would far rather choose this option.

In the months that followed, the business running the failing project was transformed. By working in partnership with the more successful project business, the team was able to refocus the scope of its work. It helped everyone figure out what each project needed to accomplish, and to document all the various commitments and expectations. Schedules were drawn up, based on the remaining tasks and resources available, together with updated timeframes to complete the revised scope.

It was clear this was the model we needed to pursue in the future. One large, umbrella business was far stronger at running projects because it had the capacity, skill and resources to do so successfully. It was also able to share overheads, which made all projects more profitable. When projects are planned and managed in one place it is easier to see the progress and recognise when one is not doing as well as it should be. The work that will make the most impact can be prioritised.

Intervening to ensure a smooth collaboration

Teams in most businesses are built over a matter of years. Individuals join and individuals leave, so the challenge for any leader is to constantly ensure everyone continues to work together effectively and commits to pursuing the stated strategy for each task. Team unity is crucial. It's what makes a group of people work together like a well-oiled machine and achieve success. If a team are all pulling in different directions, they are doomed to fail.

So how do you throw a group of people together and get them to collaborate effectively? There are several answers to this. Perhaps not surprisingly, leadership plays a crucial role in helping the team work together and realise their full potential.

A clearly defined roadmap, along with individual goals and roles, is, of course, essential. If no one knows where they are going, or who is supposed to be doing what to get them there, it is inevitable they will all get lost. And then, there needs to be good communication. Smooth team collaboration is achieved by listening to others and being open to their point of view. This doesn't mean everyone should think the same. 'Group think' doesn't make for an innovative culture. However, everyone should acknowledge, understand and respect the views of their peers and be prepared to explore all options.

Facilitating effective teamwork is often more complex than it sounds. There is so much more to it than ensuring one team member gets their ideas across to the rest of the team and interprets the views and intentions of their colleagues properly. Project teams are made up of many different personalities and temperaments and, often, I have seen individuals leap to conclusions that on closer inspection were not the right ones. People will convince themselves they are not good enough for a particular role. Or they'll decide the opposite: that they are too good. In either case, this can have damaging consequences for the rest of the team and, indeed, the project itself. If leaders want to give good direction, and help everyone give their best, we need to clearly understand any given situation. My job is to spot where these misconceptions arise and to help people realise the facts.

A leader must always think of increasing
the significance of others

A good example of this occurred with a man who was in charge of one of our large government projects. There was a challenging brief to be fulfilled and he had to lead a large team to realise a complex

35

set of goals. He came to see me one day and it was clear he was not happy. At first, he was reluctant to open up about the issue, but with a little coaxing, he spoke freely.

He had, he explained, been working on this project for some months and had invested long hours into it, day and night. He believed he was far more invested in the brief than any other member of his team.

'But I'm fairly sure that they will all try to claim the success for themselves when we finish,' he concluded.

I thought about it for a while before I responded. People are all so different and have very complex natures. Sometimes, individuals don't believe they click with those around them, or fit in well with a group. This man had a strong work ethic. He really cared about his job too, otherwise he would not have been so consumed by it. However, his attitude towards his colleagues was clearly one of suspicion, which was not healthy for any of them. The biggest problem was that he was obviously insecure about his talents, even though it was clear to everyone involved that he was integral in leading the project to a successful conclusion. It was my task as leader to help him see how important he was to this project. It was crucial that he recognised the fine work being carried out by his team, but even more important that he received external validation for his own contribution. I needed to help him adopt a new, more positive mentality. For a period after that, I made sure to give this man recognition at every opportunity. I told him over and over, 'Your work is appreciated.'

'This is my company,' I would tell him. 'I think you are doing a great job. There is no need to worry about anyone taking credit for your work.'

There was a marked change in this man's demeanour as time passed. Not only did he seem happier and more relaxed, but he also started to connect with the team around him. Once he felt more secure in his role, he found it easier to trust them and recognise their individual contributions. There is no sense in allowing members of the team to be troubled or unhappy. If one person is not relaxed, or feels anxious or concerned, there will be no teamwork. Everyone should be given firm direction and made to feel valued in their own way.

Creating a good working environment doesn't just happen. In my business, just like any other, there is a lot of work to be done, and people are busy. Even if everyone finds the work enjoyable and stimulating, which I hope they do, I accept that there are not a lot of opportunities to kick back and take some down time with colleagues. Our modern, 'always on' workplace culture, with new requests perpetually landing in our inboxes, can be overwhelming. It is for this reason that we encourage our teams to wind down and keep well-being at the heart of our people strategy.

3

The Art of Negotiation

Born to trade.

It has been said that Arabs were born to trade. While we are focused on the prize, negotiation in the Middle East is an enjoyable experience. We are always at pains to be hospitable and will treat our opposing negotiator as honoured guests. But, if they are unfair, or seek to cross us, well, that is a different story.

Ultimately though, all negotiations, whether in the Middle East or any other part of the world, are about money. When I put my money on the table, I need to focus on where a deal will take me. Will it help my business to be more profitable? The foundation for successful deal-making is to use time and energy to plan well. This is the relationship between negotiation and the mind: negotiation is an intellectual pursuit and the goal each time is to determine the value of the deal from the buyer or seller's viewpoint before the discussion even begins. Anyone who begins this process with a vague goal in mind is doomed to fail. Before we kick off any discussion with would-be partners, we spend time mapping out a clear idea of what we want to achieve and where our boundaries lie. This will include a detailed feasibility study, looking at all the options and the appetite in the market for the goods. We explore the cost implications of working with this partner for one, two and three years ahead, sometimes even more. This will take into account the various price points we will offer in the negotiation, taken in comparison to our overheads and selling price. Then, we look at the implications if the business grows, or shrinks, dramatically. What would that do to our position?

Ahead of our initial meetings, we also take steps to familiarise ourselves with all aspects of a supplier's business and consider how their goods will transfer between their manufacturing facilities and our warehouses. This level of detail goes right down to the location of the manufacturers themselves. If, say, the factories are based abroad, 20 kilometres away from the nearest seaport, what implication does this have on lead times for delivery? What is the potential for delays that could damage our business?

I am very instinctive as a business leader, but I never take anything for granted. Even when my team present me with a detailed breakdown of the agreement in question, I will always dig into it more deeply. I want to explore all the 'what if' scenarios. In other words, what will happen if the market swings another way? What if there is a downturn, how will it impact the income from these goods?

Open and honest communication is crucial so that a two-way dialogue outlining expectations about goals and financial performance is in place.

There is an old-fashioned school of thought that most of these specifics should be kept secret from the other side. The idea behind this is that it affords more flexibility on negotiating terms. I am not sure why anyone still thinks this lack of transparency is helpful. It creates an atmosphere of mistrust before you even begin. It is far better to be upfront about what you value in a negotiation. It also reduces a lot of stress, frustration and wasted time.

Sometimes, this detailed research will reveal that the deal in question is not as attractive as first thought. Indeed, it may not be worth pursuing at all. Some years ago, for example, we worked with a very ambitious retailer. We were its representative in Dubai, running a couple of shops on its behalf. Then, it unveiled plans to open hundreds of new stores in every continent.

'We want you to open a lot more shops,' they told us.

An offer like this seems exciting at an initial glance, but I was troubled. I spent a lot of time travelling and couldn't help noticing that whatever city I went to, there was always one of this company's shops on every street corner. In some high streets, the chain was opening two shops at a time, often in very close proximity. The goods that this shop sold were popular, but were they popular enough to support this level of expansion? I had my doubts. We didn't work with them on their proposed opening schedule in Dubai. Sure enough, just a few years later, the retailer began closing stores at the same rate it had been opening them because the sales simply couldn't support this level of aggressive growth.

Trust is everything

The story above underlines one of the most crucial aspects of any negotiation: trust. It is impossible to make a deal without trust on both sides. At least not a good deal. The retailer should have had more faith in us as a partner and trust our local knowledge. We were open about the fact that we didn't believe they would be successful in their strategy, as I am sure their other partners were in regions elsewhere.

Trust is crucial between you and those you do business with. All deals, even one-time deals, have consequences for the future. This is why I place such great emphasis in building strong relationships with our business partners. When both sides in a transaction fully trust and value each other, they can spend less time and energy on protecting themselves from potentially being exploited, and more on getting better outcomes for both businesses.

Trust is built over a period of weeks, months and even years, often through repeated social interactions. It is gained each time you meet face to face and through each message sent online. Every time you interact with another person, you get to know them a little better. It shapes your thinking about them, and theirs about you. It all adds up to build confidence. Once confidence between both parties has been gained, business will be good. However, even after a deal has been signed, that bond of trust must be protected at all times. Trust is, after all, the glue that holds a good relationship together.

Trust is also built on reputation. We live in a world of instant communication, where a seemingly limitless amount of information is available at the click of a mouse. If anyone wishes to do business with my organisation, they will inevitably evaluate us beforehand. So, as you might expect, we guard our reputation carefully. Our diligent approach in all our business dealings pays dividends here too. Each negotiation we make is fair to all sides and seen to be so. This is as it should be, because our credibility is at stake.

There is, however, an important caveat regarding trust. While it often feels like a special bond has been created, no business can ever simply take every aspect of a deal on a handshake. Every deal we make is backed by extensive legal agreements. We will always sit down with our partners and go through each clause carefully, one by one. This often turns into a mini negotiation of its own. *We'll agree on point one, but you will need to change points two and five in return...* While there will be a lot of backwards and forwards on this, each point is discussed on the basis of logical principle.

Avoid assumptions

The outcome of any negotiation depends on leverage – on both sides. The more one party has to offer the other one, the better their position will be. However, there is a certain amount of psychology involved in negotiation. For example, it is useful to know if one party is approaching the discussion as though there is a battle to be won, rather than basing their offer on cold, hard facts. Is their focus on a short-term deal, or a long-term partnership? Are concessions likely, or are they seen as a sign of weakness by either party?

One of the most important psychological undercurrents to watch out for is this: are both sides looking at any discussion as a meeting of equals, or is there a perceived difference in status? If one side has the idea that they are doing the other a favour, it will never end well. When there is a perceived disparity in status, it always leads to bad assumptions that will kill any negotiation from the start. Some examples include:

Where one supplier believes they are the only one capable of providing a product or service

This is never true. In fact, quite the opposite. As a business, we usually do not focus on one potential supply partner, which sells just one category of goods. We always explore the whole market, because things change all the time, particularly in the UAE, which is a very dynamic market. We always try to mix and match the range of products we buy to meet all tastes. This is prudent, so that, if one product falls out of favour at any point, there are others in the range which will sell and continue to support our profitability.

When the supplier decides the potential partner is too small to qualify for a certain pricing level or preferential terms

This is a narrow and potentially self-defeating viewpoint. A business may be small, yes, but it might have the sales platform everyone wants. It is crucial to look at the bigger picture.

Where a supplier believes a potential partner can't be trusted with key information such as profit margins or fails to be upfront about other, competitive deals

Transparency and honesty are the basis of all business relationships. As I outlined, we make a strong business case ahead of any negotiation and share our financial expectations with our potential partners. Once you begin hiding key information, the relationship will deteriorate.

Once again, one of the values that underlines good practice is respect between all parties. When this important quality is ignored, it can get a business relationship off to a bad start.

Value not price

It's easy to get carried away by the emotion involved in a negotiation. While things may look like they are going smoothly, a partner may potentially evaluate their options in comparison with other parties in the market. Their goal is, after all, to maximise their returns.

What can be done to put yourself out in front in a situation like this? The winning strategy is to add value. I am, as I have already shown, a great believer in engaging the team so we can all bring our strengths to the business. The same goes for the other side in a negotiation. Yes, we are discussing buying and selling products, but it is important to show we're genuinely interested in what they are selling. In fact, more than that, we can add *genuine value* as a partner.

Why is this important? Think about it this way. When we embark on any negotiation, both sides are looking to secure the best possible deal. We are looking to pay as small an amount for as large a slice of pie as possible. With both parties following the same strategy, it is inevitable that one of you will be forced to accept a smaller piece of the pie than they hoped.

To break free from the 'I won, you lost' notion, it makes much more sense to switch the focus away from who received a smaller piece of pie to growing the *whole* pie. This way, both parties will realise greater value from the agreement and put their offers out in front. In addition, it will deepen the bond of trust between both parties, and it will start any future discussions off on a good footing too. It is for this reason that the most effective negotiation builds the conversation around what any deal will mean to both businesses, the buyer and the seller. I find it helpful to share some of the details about how we hope to grow the level of business over the next three-year period and, all being well, far into the future. This will be accompanied by a vivid description of all the strategies that will be pursued to market the products and achieve the best possible level of sales, all using our own overheads. Similarly, details will be shared on how we will smoothly and efficiently take care of the logistics such as transportation and warehousing. The goal is to paint an enticing picture of an active business partner.

Of course, negotiation should never be one-sided. Here, skills such as listening are hugely important too. In fact, it is one of the most important things you can do while negotiating. When you listen properly, you hear what others are saying. I don't just mean the words. The tone and body language from the potential business partner say so much about what they are really thinking.

Thinking on your feet

Negotiation is always a process of thinking on your feet. Things can change very quickly, and even with all the careful preparation, you need to be ready to react. What do you do when a customer says one thing and then goes back on it? How do you deal with it when the terms are all but agreed, but then change at the last moment? Each scenario has the potential to destroy all the work that has already been put in. The potential issues can even continue once the goods are ordered when a customer changes their mind. This happens more often than you'd imagine. A significant order will be agreed, and teams set in motion to fulfil it. This process might, for example, involve pressing the button on an intense manufacturing process, or ordering modifications on goods to fulfil the client's specifications. Then, for whatever reason, the customer will change their mind. This can lead to a long and arduous legal negotiation. It is therefore crucial that the contracts we set up with clients are rock solid.

Does this break the hard-won bond of trust? A little, perhaps. I'm never one to completely relax, though, and take a relationship for granted. I know that once a bond is broken, it is almost impossible to restore, so I am always watchful. If there are ever signs a relationship built on trust is threatened, I will always act quickly.

This is something I had experience of with a supplier. We'd been working with them for a while, but despite getting along well, we could never quite tie them down to signing a long-term contract. They kept delaying and then, finally, they came forward with a proposal. They said that after a further five years of working with us, they would definitely sign an exclusive agreement.

I could not believe this 'offer'. Were they actually saying we could build the market for them for half a decade and then, only then, would we sign a binding agreement? They could very well come back after that five-year period and declare that they'd found another agent to work with.

I talked to my colleague about the situation. He'd been the person to first introduce this business to us, so I considered him to be the best-placed person to tell me more about this firm. I was then ready to speak with the principal of this company.

When we spoke, we got on well. I gave him a little background to my business, and he told me about his. But, when it came to the terms he was proposing, he was intransigent.

'We have rules,' he said. 'Our products are in demand, and this is how we do business.'

'I understand,' I said. 'But it will not be wise for me to establish the business for you for the next five years and risk you walking away at the end of it.'

My style of negotiation was polite but firm and ended with a tactful ultimatum that we were prepared to end the relationship if necessary.

Shortly after I ended the call, the firm's owner was on the phone to my colleague. He said he was getting on a plane the very next day because he wanted to meet me, as I had made an impact on his thinking.

'How can this person make a decision like that so quickly and say no?' he said.

My colleague explained this was the way I worked and that I knew exactly what I was doing, which I do. The owner arrived in my office the following day. He had only one thing to say, and that was that he wanted to sign the agreement. He wanted us to be his exclusive agent right away. The five-year wait for exclusivity was off the table.

In a negotiation like this you have to be alert. Your mind must think in all directions at the same time, and you need to knit it altogether as you speak. Most of all, though, you need to feel that you can trust the other person, and that you both have each other's best interests at heart.

There is always another, better opportunity

Read any book on negotiation and the same phrase will come up every time: 'be prepared to walk away if you don't get what you want'. I have never really agreed with this sentiment. Getting up and leaving seems much more influenced by ego than making an astute business decision. When you embark on a negotiation, you are doing so because you have worked the numbers and believe it to be a good match with your business goals. Therefore, it is better to stay in the room and see if there is some agreement to be had.

I am always patient in negotiation. I try to be far-sighted and look to the future, because an agreement won't come immediately, particularly if it is complex, or if there are sticking points. There will, of course, always be the odd occasions when a deal cannot be reached. Having done all this preparation and invested time and energy into the discussions with a potential business partner, you find you cannot get close to an agreement. In this case, the only option is to move on and weigh up another option. In these circumstances, it can seem difficult to walk away if you entered the discussion with high hopes. It's easy to convince yourself that, if you don't sign this deal, your nearest competitor may sweep in and grab it. Or, if you lose this chance, there may never be an opportunity as good as this elsewhere. However, it is never good to do a deal on the basis that it is nowhere close to what you wanted, but is the best you can get in the circumstances. When you say thanks but no thanks, remind yourself that you are not walking away from something you want. You will be walking away from something you don't want. This is the reason why you put all that time and resources into the feasibility study. The deal didn't happen because the deal didn't reflect what you wanted.

In my experience, when you do walk away, there is always something better right around the corner. In fact, one time, this is exactly what happened to me within seconds of walking away from a bad negotiation.

God, not the devil, is in the details

It was very early on after I joined the family business. It emerged that one of our international suppliers was giving us a challenging time. The company had been supplying us with their product for some years, but doing business with them was getting harder and harder each month. To start, they were slow with shipping orders. Then, this progressed to them saying they couldn't ship this or that. Finally, a message came through that they would not supply us at all, unless we exclusively devoted a large slice of our selling operation to this brand. This was getting out of hand.

I decided to travel overseas to meet with the owner of this brand. My colleagues warned me that he was very aggressive and tried to persuade me not to go, but I knew I had to.

When I met with the supplier, I understood straight away what my colleagues meant. Most meetings like this traditionally begin with small talk as both sides try to get to know one another and start to build a bond of trust. Instead, the brand owner immediately demanded that I sign a contract agreeing to buy a 20-foot container of one particular range.

'I can't sell a 20-foot container of the same item,' I said, keeping my voice steady. 'However, I am prepared to buy a 40-foot container right now, if it is filled with different products.'

The business owner shook his head and, somewhat dramatically, let out a big breath of exasperation.

'No, no, no, we will not be able to deal with you on this basis,' he said.

I kept my facial expression neutral. I was not going to give away my surprise at his behaviour.

'Okay, thank you very much,' I said. Then, turning to the colleague I had taken with me, I added: 'Let's go.'

I pretended not to see the flicker of surprise that flashed over my interlocutor's face, and I left after giving him a polite nod.

As we walked away, I could tell my colleague was brimming with questions. This was one of our major suppliers who we had been working with for years and I had just walked out. I didn't have a solution to share with my colleague right at that moment, but I knew one would come. I just hadn't expected things to happen so quickly. A short way down the road from our belligerent supplier, there was a sales office selling goods that were not dissimilar to the ones we usually bought from him. Some of the goods on display were visible through the floor-to-ceiling windows on this trade-sales-only outlet. One glance at the range told me this could well be the perfect partner for us.

We went into the shop and the manager there could not have been more charming when we introduced ourselves. As he walked us through some of their product range, it was quickly obvious that these goods were of a better quality than those at our previous supplier and could be sold for a keener price back in our region. After we agreed the basis for a deal, there and then, I turned to my colleague.

'Please go back to that man and tell him that we would like to cancel all future orders,' I said.

I could tell he was worried, but I was not concerned. He had broken the terms of our agreement. Most importantly, he had severed the bond of trust.

Of course, once we cancelled all our future orders, our former supplier immediately began to behave differently. But it was too late, and it was his loss. We didn't just place an order to fill one 40-foot container that day, as we'd discussed with him, we placed one for two containers with our new supplier. Fast forward to today and this supplier's products are still selling fast. We never did business with the original supplier again. Why would we?

4

Personal Development and Lifelong Learning

Do not ignore the person who frustrates you.
They might have something new to teach you.

To finish this section on the mind, I would like to talk about personal development, which I believe is so crucial here. To be effective as leaders, we must make the effort to learn more about what is going on inside our brain, so we can lead ourselves. It is only once we are properly in tune with our own mental energy or brainpower that we can turn our focus to leading others. We must also be resilient. Leadership is demanding and challenging. We need to protect ourselves so we can think clearly at all times and give our best.

No one should ever think they know everything, especially those in a position of leadership. We live in a constantly changing world. To be effective, leaders must be able to read the signs and predict the possible outcomes of any of these changes. We need to be constant learners, forever seeking knowledge that is both directly relevant to our field and also extends our interests outside of it. Who knows what is around the corner? We should constantly strive to become better versions of ourselves. As I often say, if you are a leader and ever find yourself thinking you know everything, remind yourself you know nothing.

Learning is a lifelong habit for me. For as far back as I can remember, my mind has been constantly active, as I have always sought to understand more about the world around me. I developed the thinking skills I needed to increase my knowledge when I started out as a teacher and progressed to become a principal of a school nearly 40 years ago, and I still find those habits useful now. Below, I have shared some of the learning skills I believe every leader should develop and practise every day.

Recognise that everything is a learning experience

Life teaches us how to behave through every circumstance we encounter. Since every circumstance is different, we are, or at least should be, learning all the time. If you are not knowledgeable, or up to date with your thinking, creativity and abilities, you will end up taking the easy path. You will just do what you've always done or reach out for whatever is there in front of you. Leading without thinking about past experiences, or without bothering about the potential outcomes, is careless. I want to be measured in my response and be proud of everything I'm doing.

Even if you are a successful leader, you must remain constantly alert and observe everything around you. Sometimes I sit and write, or read, or watch TV, but I am also always thinking and soaking up what I hear around me.

Whatever you go through in your life, whether it is hard or easy, it is all learning

Learning does not all need to be about the 'day job' either. If I am curious about anything, I explore it further. This is how I came to start learning the piano in recent years. I may not fit into the neat age profile of the usual piano student, but I find it enjoyable, and it stimulates my brain. Learning has nothing to do with age.

Read, all the time

I read something every single day, whether it is newspapers and journals or books, in both English and Arabic. My subject interests in books range from fiction to non-fiction, covering the fields of business, politics, economics, history and biographies. Each one is relevant to what I do today, even history, because our past made our present, and what we are living now will make our future. If I read something in a book that interests me, I will underline it and write notes inside the margin. (I know some people will be shocked by this, but books are there to be enjoyed and for you to get the most out of, not kept untouched, in pristine condition on a bookshelf.) I don't keep and revisit all books once I have read them, but I will keep important ones, or ones I feel I will need again when speaking at certain conferences and events. I also keep a detailed library of newspaper cuttings with information that interests me, or which I believe may do so in the future. Each subject category has its own separate folder. Occasionally, I wonder if I should throw some of these things away. However, whenever I give into this urge, I almost always need the very piece of information I have almost dispensed with.

Reading also shapes many of my decisions about the future of the business. Keeping abreast of news and current affairs, from the latest in the world economy to geopolitical developments, is crucial to making informed decisions. I am always striving to gain knowledge. Each morning, I read up on financial markets around the world, as well as the key business activities of many of the major players. For a business like ours, it is crucial to have a global perspective, as we now trade in many different countries. There are also useful things to learn from the operating styles of businesses in regions we don't currently operate in. Even if we do not have plans to open up there in the near future, there are still ideas that might improve our current business model. Plus, in a business like ours, which has a significant cash flow, it is essential to know the movement of the dollar and other major currencies. If we aren't aware of – and prepared to react to – even the smallest changes, it can make a significant difference to our bottom line. Whenever I come across something interesting, I share it with my senior leadership team via a WhatsApp group we keep entirely for this purpose.

Watch, listen and ask a lot of questions

Of course, knowledge doesn't only come from the printed page. There is so much we can learn from those around us if we are prepared to watch and listen. This has been my practice since the very first day I started working. In fact, one of my first memories of my time in head office was being fascinated by a general manager who seemed to know the numbers of our business backwards, forwards and inside out. Whenever I attended any meetings with him, he knew exactly what was going on with any part of the company. Someone at a meeting would come up with a throwaway statement about one aspect of the business and he'd pick up on it straight away. He would pull out his pile of accounts, look down any column on the balance sheet and say something like: why have you budgeted that much, when you have achieved only this much? As the meeting continued and it was obvious he had gone straight to the centre of the problem, I asked myself: *how do this man's eyes go straight to the right column?* After watching him for a while, I went to his office and asked him to teach me how to look at profit and loss accounts in the same way. My philosophy is there is no harm in asking for help or a more detailed explanation – quite the opposite, in fact. People respect that you have a thirst for self-improvement.

He agreed to show me and spent many hours helping me understand complex accounting processes, which has been a huge advantage to me as I have gone on to chair our business. This incident also shaped my philosophy of always being open to learning from people. If you feel that you are superior, or that you don't need any help, then you are the loser. It doesn't matter how much you think you know; you can always learn more. People like this general manager are invaluable.

Make time to listen to each other

There is something else to add here. Years after I started learning about accounting statements, I was invited to sit on the board of a bank. I had no foresight that this would happen one day, but I had already laid the foundation that enabled me to do the job to the best of my abilities. In this situation, just as I did with the general manager all those years before, I would ask the bank's CEO for information to build my knowledge. Ahead of the board meetings, he would send over monthly reports, so I was fully briefed on everything going on at the bank.

Learn from your peers...

In my quest to always further my knowledge, I go out of my way to mingle with those who have skills or intellectual qualities I admire. I enjoy listening to the opinions of those who think more broadly than average. I am open to taking advice from other leaders. Listening to my peers and rivals doesn't take away from my leadership. It is a powerful way to get more intelligence.

When I converse with people like this, I listen well. It might sound like an obvious observation, but in my experience, people don't often listen to each other properly. Active listening is a rare trait which I hope more people embrace.

...and don't ignore the opinions of those you may have underestimated

Here is the thing: it is not just the brightest person in the room who has something to teach us. *Everyone* has something useful to say if you are open to listening to them, even people who others might deem unsuccessful. Besides, if you only ever associate with those who are at your level of thinking, how will you ever progress? If you sit and talk with a person you don't particularly rate for one hour, it is quite likely that during that time they will make one statement that will stick in your mind. I don't go into any conversation with the intention that I'm going to need to learn this lesson from someone or elicit this certain point. I just listen and, by doing so, something will come out. You may not even notice at the time, but it could be the key to your success. One day, when you need this knowledge, you will remember that Mr A said that, or Mrs B said this. The memory will be relevant to something else that is happening right then and will encourage you to investigate and learn more. You will find it was worth spending time with that person everyone else perhaps shied away from.

Accept ideas from outsiders and study them to see what is suitable

I always like to listen to people from all levels and all walks of life. I don't need to only converse with those who think like me, or who know what I know. I need to speak with those who think differently, preferably outside the box, because I need to be outside that box too. I need to look at the world and experience different horizons. It can't just be me and my vision, not all the time. It is much better when it is me together with the vision of the people who are surrounding me.

This entire learning process is about improving yourself. The constant search for and acquisition of knowledge has so many benefits, from better self-awareness, to building resilience, to creativity. What you learn today and how you choose to improve yourself will enrich what you do in the business, making the future brighter.

Another advantage of knowledge, for a leader, is it improves their standing among their team, contributing towards building respect and trust.

I am always sure to share my knowledge wherever possible. Planning well for meetings and asking the people who will be present to send me all the associated documents ahead of the event are part of my preparations. I will then go through them in detail, picking out elements I am unsure about or where I might need more information. Then, when I am in the meeting itself, I am prepared for the questions I want to ask and the input I'd like to add. Picking up on specific pieces of information and inviting a deeper discussion are key. Once again, this builds trust, because the people there will see that I understand the issues as well as they do and have something important to contribute.

Know yourself

It is easy to think that if you have the greatest grades and are the brightest in the room, you can do anything, that it is *inevitable* you will become a successful business leader. It is not. Being successful doesn't just come from the books you read and the people you speak with; it also comes from within.

Leadership is so much more than a title or position. It is action and example, influencing others towards a common vision or goal. It is impossible to influence anyone unless they can see that you are adding value to their life. To add this value, a leader needs to fully understand themselves. Knowing yourself and the type of person you are is the foundation of authenticity. Building self-awareness and understanding your tendencies and what motivates you is what enables you, as a leader, to unlock your own potential and go on to do the same with your team.

The art of personal leadership requires a great deal of self-reflection, which means taking time to think, contemplate and weigh up a range of ideas. Many leaders find self-reflection difficult. This might be because sitting down to think about something doesn't fit in with the vision of a restless leader who is all over their brief, a constant whirl of activity and command. It may also be because self-reflection is not a quick activity and requires setting aside time for quiet contemplation. However, self-reflection is an art that all leaders should take the time to perfect. It helps you dive into the inner world of your subconscious mind, and better understand your personal motivations, thoughts and emotions and how they impact the decisions you make. Self-reflection should not be a one-off. It is a habit that requires constant practice and re-evaluation, but it is worth investing the time because it is also an investment in your team that will positively impact how you lead.

Acquiring the skill to self-reflect is useful in the day-to-day job, not just for settling the big questions, such as *What are my values?* One of my mantras is that a leader doesn't have to have all the answers, but they need to answer all the questions within them. What do I mean by that? Often, I come across challenges that I need to deal with. These are challenges that the rest of my senior team cannot help me with. When this happens, I go deep into my thoughts to 'discuss' the issue with myself. All I need is a quiet place. I ask myself a series of questions. *Why did this happen in the way it did? Why did this person do what they did in that manner? Was there a more appropriate way to act?* I find when I ask myself specific questions in this way, I discover the answers within myself. With self-reflection, everything becomes clear in a surprisingly easy way.

Stay resilient

For this final section on personal development, I have included resilience. Resilience is our ability to adapt to the challenges we encounter day after day. It helps us recover from mistakes and knockbacks. In a leadership context, resilience is a quality leaders must cultivate in order to thrive. It is important to maintain an environment where we can properly reflect on the relevant issues. We carry a great weight of responsibility on our shoulders and can be required, each day, to make a number of significant and far-reaching decisions in our role managing others. People look to us for support and courage. We set direction and build alignment. This is especially true at difficult times. Leaders need to present a positive outlook to give everyone around them the emotional strength to fulfil the strategy they've been asked to follow. We can't be seen to crumble under the strain or start making erratic decisions or over-reacting to the slightest provocation. Everyone would immediately pick up on it. They'd see the cracks and feed off that negative energy.

For some leaders, practising resilience won't be easy. It is crucial that anyone in a leadership position puts in place measures to protect themselves. If leaders do not learn how to modify their thoughts, actions and habits in the journey towards more resilient leadership it can cause lasting harm. Burnout among senior executives is on the rise. Many leaders will admit to feeling physical symptoms of stress, such as tiredness, diminished creativity, cynicism and negative thinking. If these symptoms become too severe, they can impact a leader's performance at work as they lose a sense of meaning and purpose.

A *bit* of stress now and again is okay. It's not helpful to completely banish it from your life. Stress can prompt you to deal with a difficult situation, rather than put it off until another day. It can also keep you on track to meet a deadline. However, stress cannot be left to fester for an extended period.

To be a better leader you have to lead a better, richer life

I guard my leisure time carefully. In my position, I get countless requests for help, such as being asked to chair universities, societies and charitable organisations or to mentor young leaders. While giving back is an integral part of my culture and my education, and I want to help everyone, it is not always possible. There are only so many hours in the day, and I have to choose what I do carefully, or I will burn out. Everything I do is aimed towards improving my knowledge, and then giving myself enough headspace to improve the standing of my main business.

When I am away from work, I make sure I eat well and get adequate sleep. I do my best not to muddy the waters between home and the office by continuing with my work when I am at home, although I am always ready to answer emails or WhatsApp messages from the team when they need me. The work I do at weekends is usually concerned with the charities or universities I represent, which is entirely separate from the 'day job' and does not distract from it. Besides, I greatly enjoy these extracurricular activities and they have taught me many new skills and viewpoints. When things look like they may be too much and I feel the tension and stress is getting to me, I find outlets to relax my mind and take my thoughts away from the business. I like to keep my life outside work simple. I will go on a walk or stay at home and write. Out of everything I do to keep myself calm and content, my preferred outlet is to pray. When I go to my prayer carpet, I will often sit and think about life and what I am grateful for. I might, for example, remember how our office building was built and picture all the dust there was as it went up and our pride when it was completed. If there is something significant that is bothering me, I put it in God's hands and ask for His guidance.

The other important quality that keeps me calm and mostly stress-free is loving my work. I genuinely love what I do. I realise love is a sensitive word. Many people don't like to express it publicly, but I believe it would be remiss not to highlight its importance here. Without love, there would be no understanding or interacting with others. There would be no ambitions or desire to stay involved. Love sustains my interest in what I do every day in the business, and it keeps me going back in day after day.

Perhaps one of the most important qualities that keeps me calm is finding contentment in what I do. I genuinely love working for my family business. Also, the social impact of my philanthropic interests on the community I serve is fulfilling beyond measure.

As I hope I have shown here, the mind is a crucial element of leadership. When we manage our thoughts properly, gather all the available information and adjust our approach accordingly, we put ourselves in a far stronger position to do business. However, no leader works in isolation. We also need to support and supplement these activities on an emotional level. The heart has an equally crucial role to play in successful leadership.

HEART

Emotional Energy

The heart is what keeps us alive, so we ignore it at our peril. I have long believed that our hearts guide our interactions with the people around us, and this has been a key philosophy of my leadership approach.

If our mind is the source of our intellectual energy, then our heart is the force behind our emotional energy and shapes our ability to recognise, understand and manage our own emotions and those of the people we interact with in the workplace. Emotional energy encompasses our sense of belonging and connectedness, and it shapes our vision, values and culture. Successful leaders need to follow their hearts and do what they feel is right, rather than what is expected.

5

Setting Out Clear Values

Put yourself on the path of believing in what you do and what you can do, and then lead others.

The shock on the face of one of my closest friends was striking when I told her that, after a year of mulling it over, I had made up my mind to leave my post as Principal of Zabeel Secondary School and take up a role in my family's business. She simply could not believe it.

'You will be depressed and will deeply regret your decision.'

I didn't respond to her. I'm sure that if I had, it would have set her off again. She wouldn't want to hear it, but after 14 years in education I felt I had learned all I could. I had a vision of what I wanted to achieve, and it was time to move on. Even then, with none of the experience I have now, I was of the strong belief that if you stay in the same comfortable circuit, you will never improve. To reach your full potential, you need to continually challenge yourself and seek to develop your skills.

My decision to shift from a career in education to working in my family business was not a rash one. If anything, it was one of the most considered decisions I have ever made. Some of the seeds of change had been planted by my father over many years. He would occasionally ask me, perhaps a little pointedly, how long I intended to stay in education. He then upped the ante by pointing out I had a lot of potential and should expand my horizons. Finally, he came right out with it and raised the prospect of me joining the family firm. The business, which he'd established in 1960, had grown into a large conglomerate. In 1989, his thoughts were turning to succession.

With this in mind, I had to ask myself whether I was ready for this leadership role. I had been in a leadership position as a school principal, but my responsibilities in a large corporation would be very different. To set my mind at rest, I worked through a series of questions, which I will share here:

- ○ Am I liked and respected by my existing colleagues?
- ○ Do I contribute to making them do their jobs better?
- ○ Do I have an interest in how my organisation operates, and regularly come forward with ideas on how to make it work better?
- ○ Do I enjoy learning, both about myself and about my organisation?
- ○ Am I good at building relationships and connections between all stakeholders, from colleagues to customers?
- ○ Am I a good listener?
- ○ Am I prepared to push back and say 'no' if something didn't sound right?

In all cases, I felt my responses were positive. Of course, past performance didn't necessarily predict a successful career in business leadership, but I was confident I could build on the capabilities I already had. So I told the Chairman I was ready to make the move and would work hard to develop my abilities.

'As much as I built a reputation for myself in education, I want to build a reputation for myself as a businesswoman,' I told him. 'I see this as a significant learning opportunity.'

Spend your time wisely

My challenge, now, was to decide what sort of leader I would be. As I said at the outset of this book, everybody is different, and we all make very different leaders. While I have been strongly guided by my parents, I am also a product of many other influences. My values have been shaped by the people I have met, the experiences I have had and the things I have seen. I therefore needed time to develop my own values and leadership philosophy.

Many different values combine to create a leadership style. A democratic leader is likely to value empathy and communication, while a more visionary one might value creativity and innovation, and a leader who likes things to move at a serious pace will respect hard work and responsibility. In each case, these values are led by emotions deep inside us; this is the heart side of leadership.

Leadership values affect all of our actions in the workplace. As a leader, we have many decisions to make, large and small. Some will impact a handful of people; others will affect the whole company. These decisions can be made more quickly and easily if they are first tested against a core set of values. This process will happen consciously at first, but as you get more experienced your subconscious will take over.

Values also strengthen our ability to persuade and influence others. When a leader is in touch with their values, and lives them in everything they do, they build trust amongst those around them because they are consistent in what they say and do, and this inspires people to follow their example. If you are coming from a position of authenticity and clarity, people will be drawn to your message and understand what needs to be done.

When a leader's values are strongly held, there becomes a strong element of show not tell in their leadership style. It is far more effective to lead by example than to dictate to people, which is never effective in the long term. I liken it to encouraging a child to eat unfamiliar food. If you stand over them, they will keep their mouth firmly closed. But, if you take a big forkful yourself and exclaim how nice it is, they may be curious to try it themselves.

Values are only valuable, though, when they are clearly understood and defined.

What then would my core values be? How would I shape this company? What was my vision for the future? Visions begin as images in the mind; they only become real when leaders express them in concrete terms. To begin with, I simply knew that I always wanted to be open and honest, but I was aware that I had to articulate my values more fully than that. Even when I started out in a relatively small division, leading a handful of employees, I instinctively understood the need for clarity of expectations. I couldn't simply expect my staff to follow me because I had been put in charge. Nor did I want to. I needed to establish tenets and beliefs that the people around me could buy into and build upon.

It took me a little time to articulate my list of values, but once I did, it felt like I had found my voice as a leader. The six values that follow have shaped everything about my leadership style: from the way I engage with my team to the people I hire and how I work with clients and suppliers.

Let me take you through them, one by one.

Listening

It is easy to get distracted by the people with the loudest voices when you meet with your team. You'll most likely be familiar with the scenario. When you are in a room with six people, four of them will talk non-stop. If you listen, though, really listen, you will hear that this group is often parroting back exactly what has been said by the most senior person in the room, because they want to impress the boss.

I don't go to internal meetings to tell everyone what to do. I am there to make decisions. I have very capable managers leading each one of my business divisions and I am there to hear from them. Therefore, I let everyone talk before drawing a conclusion. However, I always make a point of singling out the quieter people and asking them what they think. Maybe they are quiet because they have something on their mind. Maybe they have a negative opinion they believe the rest of the group will not welcome. Whatever it is, they should be invited to speak because they will add value. A good mix of opinions will help me come to the right decision.

If people are allowed to stay quiet and keep their thoughts to themselves, then there is no point in even having the meeting. There is no benefit in people sitting politely and contributing nothing; everyone has to actively participate. The ideas they put forward can be positive or negative, and you may completely disagree, but that doesn't matter. It is simply important that they get the opportunity to voice them.

In my experience, the contributions of the 'quiet ones' are useful nearly every time, and they frequently go on to play a crucial role in the decisions made at the meeting. When a team leader takes the time to listen, they will always benefit from broader, more honest opinions.

The listening process doesn't only happen in meetings. I make it very clear to my managers that they can come to my office and speak with me any time, one to one. I also make a point of dropping by to visit them in their offices on a regular basis. Sometimes, there will be issues they may not wish to discuss in front of the managers from other divisions. It is crucial to create a comfortable atmosphere in a private space where they feel they can speak freely. When people feel relaxed and comfortable, the conversation will flow.

I follow a similar process when I go to meetings outside my company. I always adopt a diplomatic stance: I am there to listen, and they are the experts. I may respond to show my level of knowledge so they know I understand the technicalities of the conversation, but other than that I make it clear I am there to learn. Once I have set the tone like this, people are happy to speak from the heart. They are more likely to be honest about what they need from me, or the challenges they are facing. That is the foundation of a good meeting.

Be calm, and all things will solve themselves

Empathy and kindness

Empathy and kindness are strong emotions that were part and parcel of my upbringing. Both of my parents were generous and caring people. They would tell their children that you don't win people over by shouting at them, because they will just shout right back. Instead, you should respect the feelings of others and try to understand their viewpoint. We are all human beings, and all deserve kindness and respect.

It's hardly surprising that these values became central to our family business, since we lived and breathed them at home. However, I fully believe that empathetic leadership, or having the ability to understand the needs of others and be fully in tune with their feelings, would serve any business well. While listening to one's heart and projecting empathy and kindness were perhaps once viewed as 'soft skills' in business, today's leaders need to fully embrace these values. Leaders need to be more people-focused to engage with their teams at all levels, in all departments, regardless of their backgrounds. When we are compassionate, it strengthens our connection with others. This makes us more effective communicators and leads to better outcomes for all.

Align your dream with theirs

One of my guiding principles is to always do my best to take care of everyone on the team. Whenever I speak with them face to face, I know how highly they value the multiple acts of kindness they receive. In return, I feel that they are not simply working for my company for the pay cheque. They genuinely want to be there. They really do care about the company because we have shown we care about them.

Respect

Respect is another so-called 'soft skill' that so often gets overlooked in a leadership situation. But let me ask you this: how do you feel when someone doesn't show you respect? Sad? Frustrated? Angry? Most likely all these emotions and more.

Leaders should always show their teams the utmost respect by recognising the inherent worth of the people around them. When leaders openly, or even privately, harshly judge, belittle or raise their voices at their employees, it is harmful to everyone. It doesn't matter if someone challenges me, or even tells me I am wrong or have made a mistake. That is fine. This means my team are doing the jobs they are being paid to do. What good is it surrounding myself with a bunch of 'yes' men and women? How will that help my business? I need them to help me see the bigger picture. This doesn't mean I must agree with everyone's point of view, come what may. They may be mistaken or might not know something that I know. However, if our discussion begins from a position of mutual respect, then the outcome will be far better for all parties. When you respect a person, you gain an ally.

When we recruit people, we conduct a lengthy interview process to assess their value to our business. We recruit them because of their insights, experience and knowledge, so we need to let them flourish and allow them to share these qualities with us. The only way to get the best out of people is to honour their worth, and we do this by treating them with respect.

Respect is an action. Rather than actively disrespecting someone by being rude or insulting, we *show* respect by *speaking* respectfully and *acting* respectfully.

Even if I disagree with the opinion put forward by a member of the team, I will take time to listen to what they have to say. Often, I will go away and sleep on it, so I can properly weigh up the differences in our thought processes. I frequently find that there are at least some elements of what they have said that have merit. When I meet with them again to follow up on our conversation, I will tell them this and invite them to work on a good compromise that will strengthen both our points of view. In this way, we will come to an understanding based on mutual respect, and everyone will benefit.

What I find interesting is that, when a leader models respectful behaviour, it reduces tension throughout the workplace. Everyone knows they are not going to be belittled when they speak up, so it fosters an atmosphere of calm collaboration. It is for this same reason that I make sure anyone outside the company is respectful to my whole team. Everyone has the right to be treated with consideration. When we don't treat people in this way, it is detrimental to the health and success of the company.

Leaders don't have to continually project an image of being the smartest person in the room. That is not practical, because they can't be in every room. I can't rush around each division urging everyone to follow my strategy and work cooperatively. I have to trust and respect my team enough to accept that they know the best course of action and can chart that course on their own.

Commitment

Leadership and employee commitment go hand in hand. If the person in charge of a company wants their team to be fully committed to their work, they need to demonstrate that they are committed to them as individuals. They are more than simply numbers on the payroll.

The focus should always be on employee development. In my experience, every employee wants to grow and develop personally and professionally. Learning how to do their job properly should be the bare minimum expectation for any team member. Leaders need to commit further, by providing an environment where employees can find real value in what they are doing and how they are doing it. This means helping them to grow in their roles by giving them direction and assistance in identifying how to improve. Help can be given to encourage them to see the worth in expanding their talents by creating development paths and training opportunities. This was the thinking behind our organisation's Learning and Development Centre, which provides training programmes for all levels of employees, from junior to managerial roles, right up to senior management. The standard training courses cover everything from soft skills to technical skills, with courses ranging from how to give effective presentations to finance for non-finance people. We offer employees customised sessions too. If a manager, or one of their team, highlights an issue, or a gap in their understanding of a particular element of their role, we will bring in trainers to help shore up their knowledge. We have a structured process where, each year, the business managers of each department identify the training needs of their team and courses are formed accordingly. Each employee has mandatory training hours, but there are rewards for anyone who goes beyond that, which many choose to do.

Obviously, there is a significant benefit to us as an organisation in expanding the talents of our team. A large number of our people act as ambassadors for the business. When they go out to speak with suppliers, or clients, they are the face of the Easa Saleh Al Gurg Group, representing all our interests. It is therefore crucial to develop their skills across all areas, so that they present the best version of who we are as an organisation. That being said, our key motivation is to encourage commitment and energise everyone in their efforts. A relationship like this results in a healthy allegiance to the business, which in turn translates into better results.

Harmony

When you run an organisation with multiple business units, harmony is essential. I don't mean simply that the teams should be united in their goal and willing to work together to reach it. It is also important that the managers of each department are prepared to work with each other to cooperate and share ideas. As anyone who has been in a position of leadership will likely attest, some managers don't like speaking with other managers, particularly if they don't work in the same department. There may be an underlying feeling of rivalry or insecurity about their own position. However, it is crucial to the success of any business to build a harmonious atmosphere, where everyone fully understands they are working towards the same end. In my case, in a business like ours, we are always encouraging employees at every level of the organisation to collaborate with other companies in the Group.

A leader facilitates relationship between teams

I am sure any business, regardless of size, or the presence of multiple subsidiaries, would benefit from this sort of collegiate atmosphere. Cooperation lays out the path for new business growth. Team members can help each other by sharing insights and encouraging each other. I will, however, add one caveat here. It is impossible to achieve 100 per cent harmony. While the Learning and Development Centre has been effective in training the members of the various divisions to accept this strategy and work as a community, there will always be one or two individuals who resist change. They will argue against having to work in a different way, or sell unfamiliar products, and say they already have enough challenges to deal with. They may even openly express scepticism against these carefully crafted policies. These are the types of individuals who will constantly close doors rather than trying to open them. If people like this are allowed to carry on regardless, they will eventually ruin the harmony amongst the entire team. Morale will plummet and long-term plans will fail. I am afraid there is little else that can be done but to declare a full stop and part company with managers who are consistently negative or change-resistant. Left unchecked, people like this will diminish the speed at which your organisation moves and the results it can achieve.

Interestingly, many of the other values highlighted here play a key role in ensuring harmony. Leaders need to constantly listen and observe their teams to properly understand their dynamics and individual motivations. This is how you will spot that one manager has a hostility toward another and is being obstructive.

Enthusiasm

I can't imagine anyone wants to go to work and only think about the salary they will be receiving at the end of the month. Nor can I see anyone finding enjoyment in staying in their comfort zone all the time. We all benefit from workplace enthusiasm, and when someone is excited about what they can do, success will almost always follow.

Once again, when it comes to enthusiasm, leaders should model the way. Why? Because enthusiasm is infectious. Other people see it and can't help feeling the same. It creates a positive circle of inspiration. When a leader is excited about their company's outlook, this passion will pass on to the team. Then, when the team becomes more engaged and motivated, this helps a leader sustain their own energy and enthusiasm.

Of course, I can't rely on the fact that every day will be brilliant, bringing me everything I want. Things go wrong. However, I make sure I always present a positive outlook. When leaders greet every situation with negativity, implying things can only get worse, it encourages everyone to feel the same. In contrast, if I meet any setback with a positive demeanour, presenting ideas on how to recover from it, the team tend to behave in the same way and become excited about the prospect of putting things right.

One of the most powerful ways to keep everyone enthusiastic is to cultivate a culture of ownership and community. People want to feel a sense of belonging and believe that they are working together towards a common purpose. They want to feel valued and that their contribution is making a tangible difference. Get all of these elements right and they will love what they do.

My values may not be the same as yours. They are not the same as everyone's on my team. However, they have shaped my leadership style and, I believe, given clarity to those around me. If something comes up that patently goes against my values, I will walk away from it. I won't attack anyone for suggesting something that doesn't work for me. I will listen patiently and respectfully, but then I will move on. I have lost nothing by listening, but I will have gained something by staying true to what I believe in.

6

Building Team Unity

One hand can't clap.

During my first five years in the company, I treated it like a very intense learning experience as I educated myself about every aspect of the business. I spent time in each separate division, learning the ins and outs of each one. I was determined not to come across as the owner who knew it all and didn't want to get too involved. Central to this goal was spending a lot of time speaking with the managers of each business. Leading with the heart involves being aware of the broader company vision and culture, not just one's own. I asked them what it was I needed to know. What were their challenges? Where did they need my help? Keeping in touch with my colleagues and holding regular one-to-one meetings gave me invaluable insight into the company culture and the inner workings of the business.

My training in leadership accelerated at quite a rate over this time, but even as I took on more responsibilities, I always felt I still had much to learn. In particular, I wanted to develop alongside my team. I needed their expertise to help me judge how to improve the business and make it leaner and more profitable. I was not there to simply keep it ticking over. Were there, for example, opportunities to consolidate some of the divisions to make them stronger? I began to identify areas where I could see significant opportunities for growth, such as in manufacturing and property, and through expanding to new geographies. In each instance, I sought help and advice. Who on my team knew about trading in these areas and might be best able to advise me?

I was also conscious that I needed to tread carefully. I did not want to demotivate the team or make them nervous about the future. I was not, and am still not, the type of leader to swagger in and say everyone has to do things my way.

Success does not come from one person

My first experience in leading a team was not, in fact, when I joined the family business. It was when I was promoted to become Principal of Zabeel Secondary School. Almost overnight, I was now in charge of the teachers who used to teach me Arabic, geography and geology, back when I was a young student. The big question that confronted me was, *How am I going to interact with these people now?*

I thought back to what the Chairman had often told me, which was to always respect the people on the team.

'They are integral components of the company,' he said. 'It's not you running the business alone. You have to show those who help that you appreciate what they do and give them respect and love.'

These weren't empty words. The Chairman always led by example. I had often heard stories of how he had taken the time to show the people around him the respect and love he spoke about.

I recall one time, when a new person joined as a sales manager at one of our companies. A week or so later, the Chairman made a surprise visit. This new employee didn't have any preconceptions after years of being ignored at his previous job, and he prepared himself to melt into the background as normal. To his immense surprise, the Chairman spotted him straight away and walked over to him.

'I haven't seen you before,' he said. 'You must be new.'

The Chairman spoke to this man for some time, asking him about his background and his family.

'He really seemed to want to get to know me on a human level,' the man said later.

Whenever stories like this were mentioned to the Chairman, he was always very matter of fact about them.

'One hand can't clap,' he'd say with a shrug.

He was absolutely right, of course. Success doesn't come from just one person. When a company is led by one person and it is a success, that does not mean the success is his or her success. Yes, there is success in how he or she *led* her team towards their achievements, but it was a team effort that got them there.

It was this knowledge that shaped the way I treated my team of teachers. I never once behaved like I was the boss. I treated them all as if they were still my teachers and showed them that I valued the time they spent teaching me, which of course I did. In keeping with my personal values, I was also careful to demonstrate that I respected my team as much as I respected myself.

We had a hugely successful relationship as a result. The teachers were happy, and the school thrived under their hard work. Even after I left the school and moved on to my corporate career, we kept in touch. I would regularly call or message each individual teacher to check how they were doing, even after they retired.

Trust is earned

As managing director, I continued to spend time in each division to get to know all the ins and outs there. After this time, the team I led grew considerably, in line with my responsibilities and the growth of the company itself. Even though my personal workload and responsibilities increased too, the way I treated each of the people who worked for our business was always on my mind.

So much of leadership is tied up with status. It's all about the optics: *I look like a great leader, therefore I am a great leader.* The truth is, though, the look never makes you a leader, great or otherwise. What makes you a great leader is respect and respectfulness. It is knowing how to talk and when to talk, and it is knowing when to just keep quiet and listen. It is knowing when you need to take some time to think. It is also about being approachable. If you want to lead properly, you need to be close to your team.

Remain humble and human

A leader cannot inhabit an entirely different world from their team. No matter how much you might want to, you can't do it all by yourself. You need to be able to delegate to team members and trust they have the capabilities to fulfil the company vision. To do this, the team need to have faith in their leader. They also need to feel valued in return and believe that their managers appreciate their work and are willing to listen to their views.

As I have explained, effective leadership requires a range of skills and capabilities, but there is one element that binds many of them together: trust. Trust is the foundation for stability, meaning and growth. It is also the basis for powerful and effective teamwork.

Trust takes time to build and has to be *earned*. A leader can't simply demand that their employees trust them. *Follow me, it will be okay!* I can't declare to everyone that the way I run my business is transparent and just expect everyone to take my word for granted. Everyone on the team has to see this transparency in action to figure it out for themselves.

Creating this bond of trust takes collaboration and communication. When a leader takes time to get to know their employees as people and spends quality time working with them, it always pays dividends. *Communication* is, of course, essential to any business. Taking the time to get to know a team at all levels encourages a solid, authentic, two-way relationship. It shows that a leader is open to hearing everyone's views and ambitions. It is even better if leadership is seen to be taking in this information and is prepared to act on it. Over time, all these elements will work together, helping to develop, earn and maintain trust.

Let's look at both elements in more detail.

Collaboration

Many employees are used to an atmosphere of hierarchical leadership, where the person at the top rarely steps out of his or her gilded cage to speak to those who do the hard work. However, to build trust a leader must get close to their team, showing empathy and awareness of them as individuals. To achieve this successfully, you must become familiar with each one of them, understanding their strengths, weaknesses, personal values and personalities. You need to understand what they are passionate about and what makes them tick. What is it that makes them feel like they are part of your organisation? Do they feel a sense of ownership? Gathering that credibility is the foundation for better teamwork. However, equally importantly, they need to get to know their leader.

Breaking down the barriers so the team feels at ease with this more self-aware culture can take time. At first, individuals around you may resist. They may even wonder if you are serious about them getting to know you properly. The most important aspect is spending one-to-one time with colleagues.

Obviously, I will come into contact with many of the people I manage through the day-to-day aspects of running the business.

However, there are numerous more informal occasions which are tailor-made to get to know them better, such as when travelling to trade shows, or in the 'down time' between meetings at external events. I am not only concerned with speaking with my most senior colleagues, either. I always make a point of spending time with team members at all levels. Sometimes, when people are new to the company, they seem unsure of whether or not they can speak freely with me, since they may not have experienced this elsewhere. I always make an effort to put them at ease and encourage them to express themselves. Leaders will never properly get to know their people if they always separate themselves from them.

Business trips present a great opportunity to break through that invisible barrier. When I get down to breakfast at the hotel, I take a large table and tell the receptionist that if anybody comes from our group, they should inform them that this table is our table. This first approach at treating people with full hospitality sets the mood and stops them having to worry about whether or not they should join me. This is the Arab way of welcoming others. The people who have just joined will come and sit with me and soon they will feel relaxed.

Company-wide communication

In my day-to-day job, my official interactions are mainly with the senior leadership of each division. These are the people who give me feedback and report on our progress. However, one of my priorities is to make time to go out to the individual workplaces of the companies and to speak more widely with the team there.

There are so many reasons to get to know your team better. Mainly, I want to know exactly how they think and what they want to achieve as individuals. When you understand this, it is easier to communicate your shared vision and move forward together strategically to build the business. Likewise, they will be happier to share their ideas for the best ways to achieve our objectives. Working closely together like this is empowering for the team. It helps everyone believe that they will be listened to, that their opinions matter and that they are an important part of the decision-making process.

It is not just a one-way process. I have everyone else's interests at heart too. My conversations with individuals will sometimes reveal that they might be better suited to another part of the organisation. Perhaps they have unique skills that are not being properly utilised, or they have a burning passion for something else.

Do not force unity

I don't want to micromanage my team – far from it. My goal is to ensure everyone feels empowered and fully understands that I value their skill set, be it creativity and innovation, good negotiating tactics or ability with numbers. While there is clarity on the limits of authority for each level of employee, I want them all to feel able to give the best of themselves. If that means they believe they can come to me with a bright idea or a new plan for growth, I know I have done my job well.

There is another good reason for spending time speaking with individuals from every tier in the organisation and getting to know them better: people move on. We are very careful in our recruitment process at the Easa Saleh Al Gurg Group, and this, coupled with the creative and cooperative environment we offer, means people frequently stay with us for far longer than in many other comparable companies. Nevertheless, we can't rely on anyone being there forever. Employees, especially good ones, get better offers. Or they reach retirement age. By getting to know everyone in the organisation, and their strengths and weaknesses,

I am constantly weighing up the next generation. I am calculating who will be the ideal person to move up to the next level when the opportunity presents itself. Then, should a time come when there is an unexpected gap, I can move quickly and ensure the business continues to run smoothly.

Recognition and appreciation

I want to end this section with the simplest, yet most powerful, way to build team unity. It involves just two little words: thank you. In my view, leaders cannot say these words often enough. Too many people in top positions forget to say thank you.

Saying thanks takes so little effort but goes such a long way. We all crave recognition. When our efforts are celebrated it makes us feel good and motivates us to do more of whatever it was that got us that satisfying response. It creates positivity, which in turn adds to the overall positive culture in the workplace and has an impact on everyone's engagement and performance.

When leaders do remember to say thank you, it is often in recognition for the big wins, where a tender is won or a project completed. But how often do these big wins occur? Once a month? Every few months or so? This means the words 'thank you' or 'well done' will be rarely said. What we should be doing is recognising the many small wins during that period. Thanking people on a regular basis for their efforts builds a deeper connection and a sense of belonging.

Don't forget to thank *everyone* too. Going back to the example of the big events that trigger moments of recognition, it is often the star performer in the event that gets all the plaudits – the salesperson who completed the negotiation, or the manager who organised the winning presentation. In truth, there will be dozens of other players involved in every project. Think how powerful it would be for them to have their efforts noted with a simple thank you. I always make an effort to spend time with the whole team so I can thank everyone personally. I will either drop by the department and share a coffee with them or take everyone out for dinner. During this time, I will take a moment to speak with each one individually, ask them about their role and thank them for their contribution to the company. I am very clear that this is a *team* celebration. If it were not for everyone playing their role, we would not have been able to achieve our goal.

You will note that this is not a task I delegate to another member of the senior team. As I have already indicated, I will always take every opportunity to interact with all levels within the organisation. But there is more to it than that. I believe it is crucial that everyone on the team sees that it is the leader who is recognising their achievements. This is something that cannot be delegated, or it will greatly dilute the impact.

7

Developing the Team

A leader is the message.

From my very first moment as managing director of the Easa Saleh Al Gurg Group I was constantly alert to areas where I could make a difference. One potential project caught my attention when I had noticed that a few of the villas we owned were in desperate need of renovation. Our Chairman had built them years earlier with the profits from some of his earliest deals and they were showing signs of their age. I had a vision of modernising them to make them showcases for our businesses. I went to see the Chairman to describe my proposal. He told me to go right ahead, and I contacted all the relevant people to get the project in motion. I briefed our land department about what I wanted and instructed our leasing team to inform the tenants to vacate as soon as their contracts ended. We would, I told them, give them first refusal on the renovated villas as soon as they were finished. Then, it was a question of getting the plans in place and cleared with all the relevant authorities.

When I started the process, I was confident that planning would take a matter of weeks. I couldn't have been more wrong. One month dragged into the next, and then the next, and then the next and still no planning. Meanwhile, the tenants had left their villas, which now stood empty since no work could begin. Now and again, the Chairman would casually ask me, 'How is it going with the villas?'

'It's still ongoing,' I would answer. 'The consultant is working on the plans...'

It took almost two years in total for the approvals to come through. When it did, I couldn't have been happier as I looked over the plans for what must have been the hundredth time. I went to speak to the Chairman and told him that, at last, we were going to start on the renovations. I noticed that he looked thoughtful.

'In these two years, how much money have you lost?' he asked.

'We haven't lost anything,' I replied confidently. 'The contractor worked according to the budget.'

He remained silent as he waited for me to work it through in my mind. Then the penny dropped and I realised what he meant. In my haste to get the job done, I had turned out paying tenants and the properties had remained empty all that time, earning nothing. Previously, each one of those villas had been bringing in a healthy annual income. In that two-year period, we had lost a considerable sum in rental revenue.

I was shattered when I saw my mistake. I also realised that the lesson was all the more powerful because the Chairman had the patience to leave me to work it out for myself. If he had pointed it out earlier, it wouldn't have resonated as much as it did. It was a hard lesson to learn, but a mistake I would never repeat again.

When leading a team, it may be tempting to rush ahead and give them the answers so that they achieve the strongest result every time. Do that and the team will never learn and improve. They will not feel empowered to make their own decisions or to develop their own style of leadership. Instead, they will be stuck in a permanent holding pattern, waiting to be told what to do next. Yes, every challenge is different, but what you are doing is empowering others to find solutions.

*If a leader develops their team, the team will
be stronger, and the results exceptional*

What was also interesting about my mistake with the villas is that
the Chairman never once admonished me. He remained calm and
patient. He knew how much I respected his opinion, so there was
no need for cross words. It was just important to him to know I
had understood, and he appreciated the hard work that went into
making the renovated villas a reality.

When it comes to developing the team, the leader *is the message*;
they are not only there to pass that message on. I realise now that
I used to use a similar tactic when I brought up my children. I did
not shout when they did something wrong. I would simply give
them a look, my eyes wide. They always got the message!

Help your team solve problems and create winning strategies

A significant part of any leader's job is to troubleshoot, whether
it is working out how to get a project back on track, attracting
new business or leveraging technology to make processes
smoother. The mark of a good leader lies in their approach to
solving problems. Do they have the patience to step back and
examine issues with a broad, circular vision? It is important
to be able to see around, beneath and beyond any challenge
presented, and then find a logical path through. This means
defining the problem, weighing up the options available to
solve it, evaluating those options and, finally, implementing the
best solution. Once again, we can't do this alone. Leading with
the heart involves working closely with others and respecting
their viewpoint. Any leader who tries to problem-solve alone is
unlikely to be successful.

What, though, is the optimum way to develop a skilled team and create the right environment for them to be effective? A good starting point is to always encourage team members to solve their own problems. When people approach me for advice, I am always wary of imposing solutions. It is far more effective to encourage them to come up with their own. Very often, when individuals on the team seek help with problems, they already know the answers deep within themselves. They might just need a slight nudge in the right direction, and the less direct help they are given the better. This is what happened with an acquaintance from outside the business, who came to me seeking help with a new venture she was starting up. As so often happens with new enterprises, the banks were being cautious. This would-be entrepreneur had spent weeks filling in forms and providing business plans but had got nowhere.

'Can you make me an introduction to your bank?' she asked.

While I trusted and admired my acquaintance and am always keen to help a fellow businesswoman, I suspected she already had all the solutions in front of her and was simply panicking. Starting a business can seem challenging, but if you break it down step by step it is actually quite straightforward.

I began to question her about her business and what she had done so far. When she spoke about her plans, her face lit up with passion and excitement. She told me about the fantastic team she had built around her and even began to boast a little as she told me she had a friend who was a top lawyer who she hoped might join her.

'I assume this lawyer is helping you on your applications,' I prompted.

I could tell from her startled expression that this was not the case. It was, as I expected, a situation where she had all the ingredients to do what she needed to do, she just wasn't thinking it through properly.

The entrepreneur rethought her strategy and enlisted the lawyer's help. A loan was secured and she now runs a thriving operation. All she needed was a nudge in the right direction. Giving individuals space to find the right solution, and propose their own ideas, empowers them to think creatively, develops their confidence and fosters their independence.

Empower your team and let them identify solutions

I follow the same strategy within my own business. When team members come to me and outline issues they have with their departments, or conflicts that have arisen between them and clients or suppliers, I always listen carefully to what they have to say. Then, I prompt them to share their own potential solutions. If they put forward a suggestion to change strategy, this is when I come in to challenge their thinking. I ask them to consider the consequences if we do it their way, as well as the consequences if we don't. I'll add in some further prompts of my own, digging into the detail of why their position has changed and how they came to their solution. I make them go through all their options again, so it is clear that they properly understand their proposals. If they can't answer my questions effectively, I ask them to go away and come back again when they have thought it all through properly.

When it comes to solving larger, more significant company-wide issues, communication and cooperation are key. The only way to achieve this effectively is through organisational design, so that teams across the business are well placed to collaborate with one another. This way, the most appropriate people can work on each challenge, and I have access to the best minds in the company. The term 'family business' does not need to solely refer to father, mother, sister or brother. It can also mean a close bond with *everyone* in the business.

I will give you an example of how powerful this can be. We spend a lot of time thinking about the future in the Easa Saleh Al Gurg Group. We are a diverse Group with many separate divisions. We need to make sure each division is operating at its best at all times, now and in the future. As well as ensuring the Group's overall profitability, this practice also ensures that, should one division experience a downturn for whatever reason, the others will cover the losses. Recently, we completed a detailed strategy for the next three years, and now that we have embarked on fulfilling that strategy, we are already talking about the next one. The idea behind this process is to set an overall vision linked directly to our core purpose for where we want to be in the future, but also to decide on detailed goals for each separate division in the company. These can include everything from the products they sell, to their marketing strategy, to financial goals.

Creating plans like this is not something an individual leader can, or should, do alone. Without a doubt, the people who are best placed to advise on the divisional strategies for the coming years are the general managers responsible for each one. They know first-hand the challenges their businesses face right now and have encountered in the recent past. They are also close enough to their individual sectors of industry to see the opportunities that are on the horizon, such as new tech developments. Plus, of course, they can see the threats, such as a competitor gaining ground. We have created an infrastructure where everyone in each division can contribute towards the overall vision, as well as with strategies for their own individual division. These strategies are then further broken down and explained to everyone in the Group, from shareholders to individual employees. This is done via a range of mediums, from emails to videos that have been translated into multiple languages and sent out across the Group. Our future strategy is regularly raised in meetings and our vision for where we want to take the business in the future is made clear.

Therefore, a salesperson at Company X knows exactly what they need to do to contribute to the carefully laid-out plan for the next three years.

Once again, processes like these are not just in my own best interest as a company owner; participation in setting strategic goals is fulfilling and empowering for the whole team. In the case of the general managers, for example, not only do they get a chance to collaborate on strategies that will impact the whole company, but they will also have the knowledge that their future is secure because their involvement has been integral to the company's future. They are not simply being told to implement the ideas generated at head office. We've included them at every stage, saying: we are thinking about doing X, what are your observations on this strategy? Each manager knows that their input is helping the business grow and creating a firm, viable plan for the next three years with another in the pipeline. When managers feel seen and appreciated like this, they will give more and be more positive in their work. When they see a problem, they will own that problem and work to solve it according to the vision for the future. They will take decisions on the basis that what they do will aid the progress of the company. The same goes for their team, who have the peace of mind that comes from knowing that they are working for a successful, forward-looking company that values their input.

Every employee needs a sense of purpose and an understanding of where the business they work for is going. The work we have done on setting our vision for the future has given everyone concrete plans to get behind. It also helps to shape future decisions, because they can be tested against whether or not they fit the strategy. Best of all, everyone has played a part in developing it, so it is an accurate and achievable roadmap.

Inspire others to innovate

A leader cannot be effective if they are only concerned with what they can achieve. We need to inspire others to achieve their best too. Take innovation as a case in point. Innovation is important for any business, regardless of what it sells. The strategy described above is a guiding force of where we want to be in the future, but I want the team to keep coming up with new ideas of how to get there. That is what will grow the company. Exactly how innovative the team is prepared to be will come down to leadership and the degree to which free thinking and creativity are allowed to flourish. If people are too worried about what they should or shouldn't say, or concerned that their thoughts won't be well received, they will keep their innovative ideas to themselves. Whenever anyone comes forward with ideas, I am always sure to give them a good hearing. Even if on first impression the suggestion doesn't quite add up, I help them develop what they've come up with, because no ideas are bad ideas. It makes sense to adopt a broader, more collaborative mindset. Maybe, just maybe, given the right environment, this idea could transform one of my other divisions.

Provide opportunities for people

Innovative thinking can come from the most surprising sources. I am thinking here of a young man who began his career with us in one of our departments and later progressed to work in another of our teams elsewhere. One day, he came forward and said he had great ideas for one of our divisions that was not performing as well as it had in the past. There were those in the business who were surprised that this person put his hand up for such a difficult task, but we gave him a chance. The first thing he did was to look at the products the company sold and supplement them with a new line of innovative, value-added goods. His strategy was apt, and we now sell these items on an industrial scale. This creative idea has sparked a whole array of other ideas about how we can serve a new market segment.

Dealing with tricky conversations

When it comes to leadership, simplicity is best, and nowhere more so than in communication. The goal of leadership is, after all, to act as a positive influence on people and to get them to work effectively together by providing direction and instilling confidence. If a leader's instructions are too complex, this endeavour is doomed from the outset.

This message of simplicity stands at all levels. It doesn't matter if I am talking to people in our foundries or at a major international conference. I am careful with my language. There is no point using complicated words that may elicit confusion. I want people to hear my message. The way to ensure this is to use straightforward, direct language that everyone can easily follow. This is how to get people to believe in you as a leader.

My goal is to always deliver any message clearly and precisely. Why is this important? It might be tempting to put a positive spin on difficult conversations, but that usually ends up sending a mixed message. Not only does it leave grey areas around the intended meaning, but it also leaves space for false hope. In the long run, this erodes the trust I have worked so hard to build.

If I do challenge any of my team, I do so with purpose. I don't do it because there is a clash of personalities. I know there are some leaders who challenge for the sake of challenge, to show they are in charge and all-powerful. I see no point in that. In fact, quite the opposite. I only point out errors if they are genuine problems that might endanger the business. I also do so in a way that is designed to help team members produce their own solution.

Face-to-face interaction gets things done

Leading with the heart does not mean I need to be soft-hearted, or sugar-coat messages that might seem difficult to articulate. I am prepared to deliver tough messages when necessary. I am always aware that I am leading a family business and am careful not to create a 'them and us' environment. It is not uncommon for bosses to have favourites who receive more lenient treatment than all the rest. That is something we should all be aware of, because it breeds resentment and is damaging for morale. I ensure that the simple and direct philosophy stands when there are tough messages to deliver to *anyone* in the business.

I am realistic. I know no employee is perfect. We all make mistakes and that's not necessarily a bad thing. I want my team to give me their best and that will sometimes mean taking some bold decisions, or even the odd calculated risk. When we take risks, mistakes and even failure will happen from time to time.

Managing misconduct

Sometimes, in the work environment, an employee's behaviour is so serious that it completely breaks trust between them and their leader. In this case, there is really only one option, and that is to part company. It is always a tough decision. In an ideal workplace, everyone would treat each other with respect and carry out their jobs to the best of their abilities, but there will always be a small handful of people who are not team players.

In instances of gross misconduct, the best that can be done is to act quickly and fairly. I also feel duty bound to help people understand where they have gone wrong, so they don't repeat the same mistakes elsewhere.

I will give you one incidence of where this happened, and where I believe my response had a lasting impact. The story began when I visited one of our showrooms on a Saturday afternoon. There wasn't much happening at home, so I thought I would put my day off to good use. When I walked through the large glass door, the shop was quiet, save for the shop assistant, who was sitting down talking loudly into his phone. He barely looked up when I entered, and certainly didn't seem to recognise me. This assumption was confirmed when I stood next to him and quietly said, 'Excuse me.' Instead of swiftly ending his call and attending to his customer, he held up a finger to me and angrily mouthed, 'Wait!' before resuming his loud conversation on his mobile.

So that is how things are, I thought. I wandered deeper into the store and, with one eye on the salesperson, I slipped open one of the drawers in one of the displays. After undoing the clasp on my handbag, I grabbed a large handful of small-sized products from inside the drawer and put it inside the bag. Amazingly, despite the noise I made in doing so, the man still didn't look up. I started to feel even more impatient now and picked up another product to inspect in a bid to keep myself calm. It did the trick of distracting me, because, to my surprise, the rubber seal on one side of the door came free. I had now been in the showroom for nearly 10 minutes and had still not been properly acknowledged.

I returned to the salesman and said another quiet 'Excuse me.'

'Five minutes, five minutes,' he said, gesturing impatiently.

This time, I did not wonder off. I stood beside him and waited. Eventually, he got the message and finished his call. He glared at me angrily, with no sign of making an apology.

'I want to buy this,' I said, pointing over to the product I had been looking at.

He walked over to it and pulled the door open to let me inspect it. When he did so, the rubber fell out again. I was appalled that he said nothing about it and barely seemed to notice. Instead, he continued trying to sell it to me. The item clearly shouldn't have been up for sale.

By now, I was thoroughly exasperated.

'May I ask, don't you think you should have the courtesy of ending your phone call when a customer comes inside?'

The salesman frowned. It was clear I was irritating him.

'It was a very important call,' he said with a shrug.

I had had enough. I asked him to follow me outside, told him to lock up *my* shop and call the manager. Finally, the terrible truth dawned on the salesman, but it was too late. When the manager arrived, I took the keys and handed them to him. To both men's surprise, I also fished a large handful of merchandise out of my handbag.

'These are your products,' I said. 'I stole them while this man was on the phone. He also tried to sell me a faulty item. This is not the way to look after a business.'

I dismissed the man on the spot. I didn't yell or shout at anybody. I was very calm and explained my entire reasoning for what I did that day. I had been ignored, allowed to shoplift from my own shop and expected to listen to him trying to sell me a faulty product before I closed the premises. The salesperson had shown me that he didn't care about the customer, or what was happening in front of him. There was no need for a lengthy discussion, or to drag out the process. It was clear he was entirely unsuited to working in my business. He saw the seriousness of the situation and, since it had happened just moments earlier, there was no danger of any version of events getting distorted. I am fairly confident that if he did get another job in this sector, he would never repeat the same mistake.

8

Model the Way

As a leader, remember that you are always on stage.

To evaluate yourself as a leader, ask yourself the following question: do the people around me believe in my decisions and actions? It is an impossible task to convince everyone to achieve what you want them to achieve by simply telling them to get on with it. Just because you are in a leadership position, it doesn't automatically give you authority over everyone else.

A team will constantly watch their leaders and test their credibility. Whether you like it or not, they will talk to one another, assessing what you have done, or haven't done. After all, you are responsible for the livelihood and careers of those people. They will pick up verbal and non-verbal clues looking for their meaning, and the difficulty lies in the fact that these clues will be judged according to the intentions of the person, not their position.

At the simplest level, imagine a leader has had a bad morning at home and walks into the office with a face like thunder. As they sweep past the assembled team, barely giving anyone a second glance, everyone will wonder if *they* are the source of that anger and frustration. A sales rep who is behind on their quota will begin imagining they are in the firing line and might start to think about searching for a new job. The receptionist who has been charged with giving an urgent message to the boss will be nervous about interrupting them when they are in such an obviously bad mood and they may decide to leave it until later, when the boss has calmed down. The accountant who wishes the leader a cheery good morning, but who receives no reply, will feel demoralised and ignored. *Is our financial situation deteriorating?* they may wonder. There are dozens of other scenarios like this that happen every time people try to second-guess why a business leader is not their usual self. It is, therefore, beholden upon a leader to leave any bad feelings at home. The moment I walk out of my front door every morning, I forget anything that has upset or annoyed me, and I don't think about it until I get into the car on the way home at the end of the day.

When we are in the workplace, we need to constantly model the values and behaviour we want to see. If a leader is perpetually aggressive, then the team are likely to be aggressive with one another too. Similarly, if a leader is dishonest, it signals to everyone around them that bending the rules a little is okay. However, if a leader is calm and good-natured, then the atmosphere throughout the business tends to be the same. Any team will build upon the behaviour they see at the top of the business. In the previous chapter, we looked at developing the team, and the behavioural style of a leader is integral to this process. A team will watch the way leaders conduct meetings and interact with clients, suppliers and colleagues, and they will adjust their behaviour accordingly. This is why it is so important to live one's personal values every single day.

It really is true to say that, as a leader, you are always on stage. However, it is not enough to simply give your best performance on that stage. To fulfil your role as a leader, so everyone has confidence in your abilities, you need to *genuinely* demonstrate true leadership. Remember, the foundation of leading from the heart is authenticity, and leaders need to be truly connected with their team. At the simplest level, this means showing that you are all in this together. You, as a leader, should not sit in an ivory tower waiting for everyone to get on with things.

This is another lesson I learned when I was still a school principal, working for the Ministry of Education. Exam time was always an especially hectic period, when teachers needed to prepare and mark all the exams before registering the results. It all had to happen to a tight deadline before the results were sent off to the Ministry of Education, meaning all the teachers had to stay in school until midnight during this period. At no time did a single one refuse to do this.

No one said, 'This is not my job. My hours are up to 5:30pm, why should I stay until late?'

Nor did I use my position as leader of the school to tell them to stay and finish their work. Instead, I would sit with them and work alongside them marking the exams too. We were one family. I realised, even then, that this is the environment and atmosphere a leader must create. No one on the team should feel they are being exploited, or not valued.

This may not be everyone's vision of a leader. When people talk about leadership, words such as 'visionary', 'courageous' and 'charismatic' are often listed as the qualities they admire. There is also an expectation that leaders should show off the trappings of their position at every opportunity. In my view, humility is a far more important leadership quality. Humble leaders are more human and approachable. They also make better listeners – and remember, listening is one of my most important values. Leaders don't need to show off how good they are to get the most out of others. Focusing on the team and what *they* can achieve is a far better way to inspire them towards fulfilling your joint goals. When the team around you feel their opinion and contribution are valued, they are far more likely to cooperate and collaborate.

I am not alone in this belief. In Jim Collins's business bestseller *Good to Great*, humility was one of the two most common traits among CEOs who transformed their companies from average to superior market performance. The other one was an indomitable will to advance the cause of the business.

Why do people belittle humility? Perhaps because it is mistakenly linked with the idea of subservience. There is the belief that it is a passive approach that doesn't fit with the idea of an authoritative leader. The opposite is true. Humility is a mix of highly positive qualities, such as sincerity, modesty, fairness and honesty – all qualities that comprise authenticity.

The door to success

When I first contemplated writing a book about leadership, the working title was 'Door to Success'. It was a respectful nod to the magnificent ornately carved wooden door that led into the Chairman's office. Anyone who passes through the door cannot help but be in awe of this entrance and, when my father was still alive, wonder at the great man who worked behind it. It wasn't just the grandness of the door that made me consider the title, though. The door theme has become a central part of my own leadership style, because an open-door policy encourages open communication, feedback and discussion, all key values of mine. This policy is not simply to make sure important information gets back to me; it also strengthens the bond of trust between the team.

All leaders should ask themselves what they have done to help the people who work for them. I don't mean just the big things, like providing competitive pay, conditions and benefits. I mean showing you are genuinely interested in their input. Modelling the way in leadership is not a one-off action. It is something that should be practised day after day. Creating an authentic culture requires leaders to be accessible. I pride myself on my accessibility to anyone who wishes to speak with me. If someone calls to see whether I am available to talk about an issue, I prefer not to give them an appointment for the day after tomorrow, or next week, or for some distant date in the future. I tell my secretary to make that appointment straight away if possible.

You learn from people; it can't just
be people learning from you

Everyone in the organisation has my contact details and is encouraged to use them. And they do. Even if I receive an important email late at night, I will respond. Technology enables us to work more efficiently, so it seems wise to use it to its full potential. As far as I am concerned, the quicker I respond, the quicker things will get done. If I can't deal with the request, I will always forward it to someone who can help.

There are multiple advantages to an open flow of communication. From a business point of view, it activates an 'early warning' system, where the team can quickly alert me to any issues that might be coming up. These issues might not be immediately obvious to everyone, but left unchecked they can grow to be damaging. Plus, of course, it is much easier to deal with a problem while it is still small. An open-door policy also encourages a flow of new ideas by promoting healthy and constructive discussions. It also provides an outlet if anyone faces challenges that they cannot cope with independently or has a clash with another member of the team, or simply feels isolated.

The close ties I feel with my team work both ways. Because I consistently demonstrate that I would go out of my way for them, they are more willing to do the same for me. This is, at least partly, why people stay so many years with the business. It is not unusual for our employees to be with us for 25, even 30 years, whereas it is increasingly common for people in our industry to jump ship every two or three years. It is also why I see people prepared to work long hours when a job requires extra input. Similarly, when they are out of the country on holiday, my team will call in to check on the progress of projects. This is not a company rule. I have simply modelled this myself and done my best to create an environment where there is a close harmony between everybody. Everyone feels like they are a part of something, and this is how to make things happen. If I was not fair to my company leaders and didn't treat them well, I would not be where I am today.

Loyalty is non-negotiable

In authentic leadership, loyalty is crucial. Loyalty is where we establish lifelong connections based on respect, trust and credibility. It is earned by modelling the behaviour I have outlined here, which prioritises the emotional interests and needs of the team and encourages a regular two-way dialogue so everyone can reach their full potential.

Loyalty works both ways. While I will do everything in my power to champion my team, and to be seen to do so, I also value loyalty highly and expect them to be loyal to me in return. I expect my team to stand alongside me, just as I do all I can to stand alongside them. I do not want to work with people who are not honest with me, and I am transparent about this. When people make a mistake, I will always do my best to help them, as long as they are open about it. However, people should not confuse my desire to work in a collaborative environment, where we can all be our best selves, with me being a soft touch. My goal in working alongside my team is purely to create the conditions in which we can all be our best selves. That is why, to me, the non-negotiables in business are integrity, a good work ethic and loyalty.

Dealing with tension and stress in the workplace

Any leader who says they are not personally impacted by the stress of their position is not telling the whole truth. However experienced you are, and however on top of the job you claim to be, there will always be days when the unexpected happens, or someone lets you down, or a small problem suddenly becomes very big indeed. Days like this will take their toll.

I am not impervious to stress, but I understand the dangers. There is a real chance high levels of stress can have a negative influence on your leadership. As outlined above, the fall-out from a bad day may well be misinterpreted if the team sees their leader looking angry, sad or worried. Plus, if a leader is permanently stressed, their team will operate with the same knot of tension in their stomachs. That does not make for a relaxed work environment.

Use your mind. Don't let your mind use you

We all experience stress, but it is how we deal with it that counts. When I am faced with a big problem, my preference is to take myself away from it for a short while. I will go away from the source of the stress and spend time in thought. I will frequently take a sequential approach, working my way through the issue to give myself an understanding of how we got to this point. This separation from the moment of tension, along with more measured thinking time, will frequently reveal a solution that was lost in the heat of the moment.

Even in intensely difficult situations, I tell myself it is better to keep my composure. I am very conscious of the inner voice we all have, the one that tells us something is much more worrying than it actually is, or that something needs to be dealt with *right now* or it will become a significant threat. The mind is important, but it can be stubborn and aggressive. It can push you into knee-jerk reactions, when acting on impulse is not in your best interests. When I feel that this may be happening, I repeat a short mantra to myself: listen to the voice in yourself but direct it. In other words, use your mind, but don't let it tell you what to do or force you to ignore the feelings in your heart. Ideally, heart and mind should work together, particularly in difficult situations. Neither should be allowed to dominate. There are always other options to consider if you step back and give your heart and mind room to figure things out together.

I am, by nature, a positive person. It is easy to respond negatively, but seeing the worst in every situation only causes more stress. I make a conscious effort to deal with stress before it intensifies, to prevent it from disrupting my life and business.

Alternatively, I won't think about the issue at all. I will occupy myself with something else entirely, a relaxing activity such as drinking coffee, or watching a film. Amazingly, when I step away for a short time like this, a solution will usually present itself.

Many leaders say they find themselves short of time, which can add to the stress and create tensions in the workplace when others pick up on it. I don't feel that way, but this is a result of deliberate actions that I take. I use every second to the fullest and am specific about what I do.

My tips on being efficient and managing my time carefully are as follows:

- **Don't procrastinate** - Never leave something that can be done today until tomorrow, or the day after. Everything that comes in goes out the same day. At the start of my working day, I deal with issues that have come in overnight.

- **Be organised** - When I leave the office at the end of each day my desk is tidy. When I am not in the office and things are sent through to me, I deal with them as soon I see the alert on my phone.

- ○ **Prioritise** - I constantly receive requests for meetings. It would not be productive to spend my whole working day in meetings, so, depending upon my capacity, I prioritise some, which are invariably those concerning my business.

- ○ **Stick to the schedule** - When meetings do happen, I'm always on time to these meetings and expect people to show me the same courtesy. I am very clear up front that I only have half an hour, or however long has been allocated to the meeting.

- ○ **Plan ahead** - Before any meeting, I always request an agenda. This means that during the meeting I know what to expect and can get straight to the point.

- ○ **Delegate** - I don't make the mistake of thinking I need to do it all. A leader needs to have the right talent and support to be able to delegate tasks.

It is not just a question of being efficient. I find working in this way also reduces stress. I become restless if I leave tasks 'for later' or feel things have become disorganised. My mind starts thinking, I should have done that. If I leave nothing to do, I have nothing to trouble me. If I do find something is beginning to trouble my mind, I deal with it right away.

9

Facing Challenges

Remember the importance of humility.

To gain and maintain the respect of the team, a leader needs to do more than just lead. In this final section on leading from the heart, I would like to discuss the importance of humility. While it is important that leaders are always ready to share successes with everyone involved rather than claiming the glory all for themselves, it is equally crucial to 'own' any failures. While many leaders find this difficult, humility is an important component of authentic leadership.

In recent years, there has been more acceptance of the value of failure. At a corporate level, people understand processes and practices won't always go as expected. When you are pushing hard, taking calculated risks and being innovative, things will go wrong. Mistakes will be made, but they show that the effort is there, along with the will to succeed. There is, however, a reluctance to discuss any failings on a personal level. Leaders, in particular, shy away from talking about any perceived weaknesses in case of a loss of esteem or stature.

Leaders need to be more open and tolerant about discussing failure, to encourage a culture of intelligent risk taking. It is part of a more human approach that engages at a personal level with the people they lead.

Forget fear

There is not a person in the world who doesn't feel fear now and again. Somehow, though, a myth has grown up in some quarters that leaders don't feel fear. *Leaders are heroes!* But all leaders feel fear at some point. In my view, those who say they don't are too swept up in how outsiders look at them.

Leaders are prone to the same stress, anxiety and difficult emotions as everyone else, plus perhaps a few more since they are in a position where everyone is looking to them for guidance and support. When I take decisions and agree to invest a large sum into a project that may take two or three years to realise a result, I can tell you that my fear is there. There is a voice inside me that pops up to ask, *Are we on track?*

The rational side of me says that of course it is going to go well. As I have shown here, we don't take decisions unless we have carried out a thorough feasibility study. And for significant decisions involving large projects, well, as you might imagine, we are very thorough indeed. Even so, the fear is still there, proving fear is not necessarily a rational emotion.

If you are reading this and are in a position of leadership, here are a few fears you may recognise:

Fear of not being good enough
This is especially common in challenging leadership roles. Also known as 'imposter syndrome', it is where someone struggles to believe that their success is deserved. They feel they are not the right person for the job and worry they may be found out.

Fear that other people can do the job better
There will always be people who think they can do a job better than the person in charge, and it can be easy to start suspecting they might be right and constantly question your own decisions.

Fear of not providing enough value

Leadership roles, particularly in large organisations, cover a lot of ground. There is so much to deliver across so many different parts of the business that some leaders feel they are adding no real value in any area. This fear can be further amplified if there is a highly competent team of managers in the layer below. Leaders may wonder whether they are needed at all.

These fears are usually completely unfounded. *Imposter?* Then why did you get the job in the first place? *Someone can do the job better?* That's a healthy part of corporate culture because it shows individuals are ambitious and keen to progress. Personally speaking, I am more than happy when I think my team are capable of getting on with things without me, as it shows I have empowered them.

Fear itself is not a bad thing. It is a natural part of leadership and, in many ways, as important as confidence. It keeps us on our toes because it challenges us to be more thoughtful about our actions. When I feel fear, it encourages me to re-evaluate my decisions and stops me from becoming complacent. However, I won't allow it to change what I do if the evidence shows that our actions are running entirely in line with our carefully written strategy, particularly since that strategy is fully backed by data from a feasibility study.

What makes the difference here is when fear is allowed to take over and makes decisions irrational. If a leader ignores all the available evidence and gives in to this intense emotion, it can be more damaging than the fear itself.

When a response to fear is badly thought through, it generally falls at either end of a spectrum. Leaders will either avoid whatever issue it was that stirred the strong emotion, or they will overcompensate. Both responses are equally damaging and will impact a leader's performance. If someone is suffering from imposter syndrome, their fear of being found out may hold them back from pushing forward confidently with their agenda. Instead, they might take a series of smaller, weaker steps. These steps won't achieve what is required, and the team around them will be less motivated because they will instinctively pick up on the under-confidence of the person in charge. Or, at the other end of the scale, a leader will overcompensate for their fears, taking huge leaps forward in a bid to seem like they are taking control. This dramatic option won't just be seen as over the top and domineering, it will alarm, intimidate and unsettle the team.

In both cases, this is a completely inauthentic form of leadership. Trying to appear to be something you are not is not only tiring and stressful, but it also alienates the team. If a leader is not 100 per cent honest, it puts pressure on those around them to suppress their own challenges. The same goes for any of our irrational responses to fear. If, for example, a leader is always entirely upbeat, even when things are clearly not right, it undermines their relationship with colleagues. Similarly, if a leader is masking their fearfulness by being overly aggressive, they will be completely out of tune with those all-important softer skills that create a cooperative working atmosphere.

It is complicated running a business, but leaders need to be steady and thoughtful and maintain the direction they have carefully mapped out. This doesn't mean that the person in charge should insist they feel no emotion about the outcome. Being honest about negative emotions such as fear, or nervousness about a project, builds empathy. It shows others that you are as fully invested in it as they are and encourages them to be more open about their feelings too. This is what sets off those more human conversations, where everyone on the team feels more comfortable sharing ideas, or concerns.

It is always better to note one's fears, and then adopt a measured response, taking steps to work with those fears. Very early on in my leadership career, when I found myself being regularly asked to speak at large events, I was nervous about these appearances. They would often mean standing up to deliver a speech to hundreds of people, as well as making myself available for question-and-answer sessions afterwards. As I described in the introduction, I would practise in front of my family so I could give my best performance on the day. I found this took the edge off my fears. I also got into the habit of asking the conference organiser to provide me with a list of questions they anticipated I might get, so I could begin to formulate my answers. This list couldn't be exhaustive, since the audience might take a different approach, but it helped assuage my fears. This has started a lifelong practice where I always prepare meticulously for any and every event, whether it is a company-wide town hall talk, or a public speaking engagement. Thinking about it now, I can see this is a similar practice to our in-depth feasibility study. When you have thoroughly covered all the angles beforehand, it is a lot easier to be confident.

Dealing with mistakes

The big question, as a leader, is, *How do I deal with it when a member of the team makes a mistake or a strategy doesn't go as hoped?* My starting point is to acknowledge that mistakes are never made intentionally. A mistake is a mistake. It is impossible to run the world in exactly the way you would want to. Likewise, a leader can't be on top of absolutely everything that happens within their organisation, because we have charged our teams with carrying out the strategies we've designed. Dealing with problems and mistakes means we need to put aside our judgement, anger, guilt and self-directed feelings, and replace these negative reactions with a desire to help others.

I always encourage people to see beyond simplistic definitions of failure. Failure is not the opposite of success. It just means something someone tried to do didn't work out. If a leader's first reaction is to admonish when they hear that something hasn't gone as expected, they shouldn't be surprised if:

(a) no one ever tries too hard, or

(b) they don't get told about mistakes.

When a glass is broken, why shout about it?
The glass is not coming back

When you view mistakes, or indeed any challenges to a business, with a calm state of mind, it helps you see things in a very different way. When one of my divisions suffers from falling profits, there is no point hauling the manager in front of me and aggressively demanding an explanation. I am fairly certain that they have been thinking about little else for most of the year, worrying about how to improve the performance of their division. How will my adding pressure to the situation change things for the better? It is far more useful to have a calm, productive discussion.

Often, by remaining calm and probing carefully, I find that people tend to overexaggerate the consequences of something that hasn't gone well.

Leaders often feel a compulsion to jump in, act quickly and correct a problem before it builds up and gets worse. When I was younger, I used to do just that. Whenever there was a problem, I used to try and sort it out immediately. Experience has shown me that it is better to leave it for a short while. Any significant, or potentially significant, issue in the business may well require a big decision to be made and needs adequate time for reflection. Success, or otherwise, in solving problems depends on how the circumstances around the problem are tackled. One should never confuse acting swiftly with acting effectively.

Clearly, some failures are very significant and will need to be dealt with properly. Anything that might threaten the safety of others needs to be swiftly and definitively dealt with. Similarly, anything that threatens the ethical integrity of the business needs to be dealt with immediately.

What, then, if an initiative falls short of its expected goals, even though the entire team has apparently been giving it their all? There are a number of questions I'd ask before I jump in to criticise. It could well be that the team was doing everything right and stretching themselves to the limit but something unexpected intervened. I would explore the issue by comparing the actual costs and outcomes of any project that didn't succeed as expected with the projections of the feasibility study. Was there a case of over-optimism when the study was drawn up? If so, what could we learn from it? I'd also ask if the team had followed the original strategy and remained true to its goals, or whether corners had been cut. Was there an issue with collaboration? Did someone involved in the process resist working alongside colleagues?

This approach is not an attempt to micromanage, but merely to encourage the team to think more deeply about their own roles in whatever has not gone to plan. It prevents any knee-jerk explanations, or swift judgements about the potential causes of the issue. When we don't jump to conclusions, we leave space for everyone to learn more about what went wrong. This non-judgemental approach opens the way to teach people how to thoughtfully pursue ambitious projects in the future and can become a productive part of the learning process. By learning what doesn't work, we can focus more on what might work.

Once I have a good idea of what has been going on, I move the conversation on to exploring areas for improvement. Ideally, this will open up a productive discussion that will lead to meaningful progress.

I believe that success should be analysed in a similar way. When an initiative is an unexpected runaway success, far exceeding our expectations, I'd ask, *Why?* These exceptional results may be the outcome of a brilliantly planned and executed strategy, but we won't know that for sure unless we investigate more closely. Sometimes, success is the result of fortunate coincidences, a product of being in the right place at the right time. That is great, but if you ask the right questions, so you know more about it, you can make sure you stay in that place for longer. The questions can be quite similar to the analysis used for projects that don't go so well. Why did the results so exceed forecasts? Did some people contribute more than expected?

When this analytical response becomes embedded into a company culture, it encourages everyone on the team to be more collaborative and to speak openly and frankly. The focus here is on increasing knowledge. It helps everyone to be analytical about any mistakes that are made, as well as successes, which increases the experience, knowledge and creativity of the workforce. It also helps everyone to readily accept accountability, as well as use their expertise to correct the problem.

Clearly, if the same person continues to make regular and abundant mistakes, a slightly different conversation will need to be had. High-performing employees will make more missteps than their less ambitious colleagues. It is part of the process of rapid growth. However, each mistake does need to be noted and carefully reviewed, and there may be a call for training in any areas of weakness.

Realising opportunities out of adversity

Businesses face disruption all the time, but it is how we adapt that differentiates us. As the previous section outlines, my interest lies more in what we can learn out of adversity than in admonishing people for the fact that it happened in the first place. To conclude this section on dealing with challenges, I would like to touch upon one of the most significant challenges that any business around the world has had to deal with in recent times: the pandemic.

When the virus began to spread, the response of the business community was swift. To explain how our organisation adapted, I will highlight the story of one sector in particular: retail. Many businesses the world over with a large exposure to retail responded to lockdown by letting go of a significant part of their workforce.

We had a big decision to make. For years we had made much of valuing the team and their input, yet with all the malls shut, this side of the business was not bringing in any sales, not to mention it was costing us a great deal to keep ticking over. My response was to remain calm. My business had been through challenging times in the past and I knew we were well placed to come out of it okay. Most of all, our core belief in our team had not changed. We wanted to do what we could to protect them and ensure we all came through this together.

After evaluating the circumstances, we decided to keep the entire team on the payroll. We had an internal communications campaign to reassure our team and to provide clarity for the future.

'We are all here. We are all one family,' we said. 'We all support each other. If there is anything you need, we are always here.'

For those team members who were stranded abroad, we told them to extend their vacations until they were able to travel back. In the meantime, we turned our attention to our new circumstances, moving much of our operations online, so we could ensure the businesses kept going. This way, once it was all over, everyone would have something to go back to. From an almost standing start, we actually achieved a record month at the height of the pandemic. This enabled us to return to business as usual when everyone came back to work, with minimal disruption to our operations.

Our success in keeping the team and finding innovative ways to trade in the digital world was down to the agility of everyone and their ability to work together in a crisis. But we helped create the right environment for them to do this by quickly taking the stress out of the equation. They knew they had a job to return to and their livelihoods were secure. Since they were calm, it led to a high level of productivity, which was in all our best interests.

Now, as we move into the recovery phase of the pandemic, we need to seek out and examine the opportunities we found in this difficult period. We gained some useful insights into our customers' priorities during this time and it showed us better ways to deliver our products and services to them without compromising on our values. It reinforced the value of collaboration between teams and led to a big step forward with our digital capabilities, both in terms of creating a safe and productive working environment and creating a new revenue stream in our consumer-facing businesses.

At the simplest level, the pandemic also helped us discover many things we could do without. Whereas, previously, we used to travel around the world to meet with customers and suppliers, we now conduct more meetings in the virtual world. This cuts down considerably on what we spend on air travel and hotel expenses. It also means we can be more reactive. If a potential new partner from the other side of the world wants to meet with us that afternoon, we can make it happen. Yes, it does sometimes take away some of the human touch, but it is a question of finding a better balance. We still make the journey where face-to-face interaction is absolutely necessary.

A proportion of our team have switched to a more hybrid working model (Friday is a work-from-home day), in the same manner as countless other businesses. The flexibility suits some people who have family commitments. We don't mind this, because we have discovered that people who prefer homeworking are capable of working just as hard and have demonstrated their ability to take responsibilities for their own schedule.

At a deeper business level, we have had to reassess internal processes and structures to improve efficiency and, in particular, look at our supply chains. Many of our manufacturing facilities are reliant on imported materials. There were widespread shortages during the peak of the pandemic, and we anticipated that this would continue in its aftermath. We have adjusted our practices to plan ahead and order greater quantities of raw materials where required, so our manufacturing capabilities are not interrupted.

Overall, I believe the pandemic made us more resilient as a business. Like every other company, we were thrown into the midst of fast-moving events that were beyond our control, however our culture of learning and adapting meant that we emerged stronger from the crisis. Our teams showed that they could work together, quickly and efficiently, to resolve some difficult challenges. There is no way to plan entirely for the next major disruptive event because we have no idea what it will be, or how it might impact us as a business. However, recent experience has taught us to work together to plan and prepare for the next inevitable disruption.

Leaders who understand the importance of the heart, allowing themselves to lead with emotion while recognising the power of their vision and values, will connect more closely with their team, and together they will create a winning culture. This guiding philosophy will build upon what they achieve by attending to the mind, and the intellectual energy behind their leadership. Now, for the final section, we will turn to the legacy of our leadership endeavours. The soul of our leadership centres around what we leave behind, and how we shape and strengthen our organisations to move into the future.

SOUL

Spiritual Energy

There are many interpretations of the word 'soul', but most refer to the spiritual part of us. In the context of leadership, I like to think of the soul, or this spiritual energy, as something that comes from knowing who we are and why we are here. Thus, the focus of leadership in the context of the soul is on something bigger than ourselves. It is the legacy we leave and the meaning the organisations we shape give to all the people whose lives they touch.

Businesses have a soul too. It's the energy that runs through them, shaping the culture and the direction of decision-making. The soul of a business is the shared goal that drives everyone within it to continuously forge new paths, come up with ideas and find success. It is what helps a business to be a positive influence on everyone whose life it impacts – employees, customers, suppliers and stakeholders. For a company like ours, the soul of our business is at the core of everything we do.

The soul of any business is shaped by its past but nurtured by its present and carried forward into its future. Leaders play a crucial role at every stage.

10

Building a Talent Pipeline

Do not keep your knowledge locked in a box. Share it.

Leaders need their best people around them to shape and protect the soul of the business. It works the other way around, too. With an ever-watchful eye on the future, it is also crucial that we look after our senior teams, particularly those with the strongest chance of becoming leaders themselves. It is our role to help them to develop and move forward into the positions they deserve.

Employees at all levels stay with an organisation out of choice. It is therefore beholden to leaders to create an environment where everyone feels valued, so everyone on the team wants to be there. A great deal of this will be down to how they feel about working for the company. Do they believe they can thrive within the organisation, or do they feel the best they can do is survive?

A thriving workplace is one where:

- ○ People enjoy what they do and are fully engaged with it.
- ○ The team can see the bigger picture and their role within it.
- ○ Everyone feels empowered to do their best work.

What brings all of this together, cultivating a thriving workplace, is inspirational leadership. This doesn't simply mean one inspirational figurehead at the top. It means creating a pipeline of inspirational leaders that runs through the whole organisation, engaging the team at all levels and empowering them to use their skills and abilities in the most powerful way.

Caring is leadership

Recruiting a new generation of leaders

As I stated right from the start, no two leaders are the same. While all recruitment decisions are difficult, getting it right when choosing the senior leadership team is one of the most difficult tasks a leader can face. The team at the top of any organisation have a significant impact on so many things, from the strategic future of the business and team morale to the depth of connection with our customers.

What, then, should a leader look for when recruiting their senior teams? It will probably come as no surprise to you that I look for people who have similar values to my own. While qualifications and experience are important, it is crucial to look deeper than this when weighing up candidates to join the highest level in any organisation and to work across individual departments. As the title of this book suggests, authenticity is key. I want to be surrounded by people who are genuine and open, and who have the ability to inspire the team and build trust.

In addition, I look for qualities that clearly signify this person can become an outstanding leader given the right guidance and opportunities. It might help to break down the qualities I think any leader should prioritise when recruiting a senior team.

Over and above traits such as passion, integrity, honesty and thoughtfulness, some demonstration of the following qualities is essential.

Strategic thinking

It is only natural that an interviewee will be keen to talk about their accomplishments and describe why they are the perfect candidate for the role they have applied for. However, I am always wary if, during an interview, a person insists they are the exact fit. If an interviewer asks if the candidate is up for the challenge of turning around a failing business, the response they don't want to hear is: yes, I am 100 per cent ready for it. This suggests the opposite may well be true.

A more appropriate response might be:

'I would like to take some time to study this business properly and get more deeply into what has been happening there. I see that there is a six-month probation period with this position. Give me six months and then I will come back to you with a proposal. I'll tell you where I think it has gone wrong and will propose the strategy that I believe is necessary to repair it. I will also give you a detailed breakdown of the costs involved to turn this from a loss-making business into a profitable one.'

The difference between these answers is huge. It is not that supremely confident people are not good leadership material. They are. However, candidates need to *think* before they respond. The candidate that gives a full answer explaining how they are going to properly interrogate the issues that have been highlighted is not just telling the interviewer what they think they want to hear. They are giving a considered response.

Enquiring mind

Any candidate for a senior leadership role should be well read. I don't mean they should have digested every business and leadership book known to man. I respect people who have a thirst for knowledge about *every* subject from history to economics to geography. I appreciate an enquiring mind because it tells me a lot about a person and their leadership style and because it always translates well into a business setting. It shows that a person is on top of what is happening globally and is, therefore, better placed to judge what our customers will want in the future. They will know which regions of the world are up and coming and good to trade with, versus those facing issues that might negatively impact future business. When a leader is looking towards the horizon and is fully aware of their surroundings, they are better able to think outside of the box. They are also better equipped to engage with their teams and help them to achieve the strategy that has been carefully set out.

Self-motivation

I'm always interested in what motivates other leaders. There is a school of thought that says money is the simplest and most powerful motivator. Ergo, the more money we get, the harder we work. While money is, indeed, an incentive and many might feel that earning more would make life easier, I would be wary of someone who clearly only comes to work to get paid. It's incorrect to think that if I gave someone 20 per cent more money they would work 20 per cent harder. The most effective leaders are motivated by a wide range of factors. I like to see enthusiasm for the contribution they might make to the company's overall success and excitement around the responsibilities they are charged with. It is also good to find people motivated by the idea of career progression.

Communication

Effective leaders interact with others in a way that feels genuine. This doesn't mean they need to be extroverts. Introverts make good team leaders too. Being a good communicator simply means showing empathy, engaging in active listening and having an ability to build strong relationships.

Anyone aspiring for a senior role needs to be well versed in the figures too, so when they go into meetings they can speak confidently and knowledgably about financial issues.

Perseverance

When you hear the story of any successful individual, a common trait will always emerge: perseverance. This is the ability to stand up and take a step forward when most people would sit down. There are many examples of individuals who have progressed and grown in business because they have come across obstacles and not given up. Instead, they have invested their time and energy in finding a way through, or around, them. If you were to break down the qualities that fuel perseverance, I would say that a clear sense of purpose is essential, as is a desire to make a change. I also believe that willpower is required.

In any interview situation, everyone will be on their best behaviour, but it is important to look through that. It helps to focus on tone of voice and vocal delivery, since it is quite difficult to hide an undercurrent of aggressiveness, which is not a good trait. Likewise, body language speaks volumes. It shows whether the candidate is confident and honest, and fully involved in the conversation, or uncomfortable and even hostile. When a candidate is authentic, it always shines through.

While a candidate should share the values of the organisation they hope to join, it is healthy to have a mix of people in any business. Good teams are represented by a range of qualities, skills, experiences and outlooks. It is this breadth of perspective that adds up to stronger, better decision-making, because everyone will challenge each other's thinking. Also, if an individual is strong in one area but weaker in another, another member of the senior team should be able to compensate for this. There may, for example, be one team leader who is very ambitious, while another is quite cautious. If they work together, they will complement each other's strengths to create more considered results.

Developing future leaders from within the company

I am often asked, *Is it always essential to bring in senior talent from outside?* Most definitely not. The grass is not always greener outside any business. For this strategy to be effective, as we have said, a pipeline of skilled, highly prepared leaders and managers needs to be built inside the company from the ground up.

A leader creates other leaders around them

Not everyone is leadership material. It is not a given that if a person does well in their department and is promoted to a more senior position they will automatically become an inspirational and effective leader. The skills required to lead even a small team are different to those needed to manage one's own day-to-day workload. Some people will not grasp them as easily as others, and each successive promotion will require an entirely new set of skills. It is crucial that the requirements for each new level of leadership are properly understood, so the leadership in any organisation can provide support to those moving up the ranks: mentoring, coaching or any other assistance deemed necessary.

Transitioning to a position of greater responsibility requires assessing one's existing soft and hard skill set. By going through a process of self-evaluation, each person is best suited to seek the tools they need to move up the career ladder. To explain this a little better, let me break down the various tiers of leadership to illustrate the different skills people require as they progress from one stage to the next. The degree to which this matches your own situation will depend upon the size and nature of your organisation.

Tier One: Managing oneself to managing others

Transitioning from a position as an individual contributor to one where there is a need to lead others is always a significant career milestone for the person involved. Think here of someone who is, perhaps, a sales associate or a junior accountant, who is then promoted and put in charge of a small group of sales associates or junior accountants. Previously, when working solo, this individual will have been given tight timeframes to meet clear objectives. Now, because they've proved to be adept at their first job, they have been rewarded with additional responsibilities. For the first time, this person will be in control of getting work done *through others*, rather than just managing their own workload. A whole raft of new skills must be learned, from making time to speak to and motivate their new team, to planning rotas for the weeks or months ahead, to measuring workflow.

Tier Two: Managing others to managing managers

This is another crucial tier, which takes people into new territory. It is also here, for the first time, that those who might become future company leaders begin to emerge. The individual task element that was still present in Tier One largely disappears and, here, managers will only manage. One of the biggest issues presented by this step up the career ladder is that it is often assumed, since an individual has already led a small group of people in Tier One, their managerial skill set is already established for this progression. The task here though is quite different from the 'managing others' role. In this next level of leadership, the key new skill that needs to be mastered is identifying the next generation of managers. This is more difficult than it sounds, and often those who have done well in Tier One are best suited to remain in Tier One.

Coaching is helpful at this stage, to help managers take responsibility and 'own' the success of the people being managed. Strategic thinking skills can also be introduced, as well as advice on how to take into account the requirements of the broader organisation.

Occasionally, it will be necessary to take a leap of faith with certain members of the team. They may have some of the skills required for the next level, but not all. However, the skills they have and their passion for the job could make them intriguing candidates. This takes courage because the stakes can be high, but it is something I am not averse to trying now and again based on an instinct that some people will prove to be exceptional leaders if they are just given a chance to shine. Get it right and your business will take a big move forward. To describe how powerful this can be, let me give you an example.

When I did my regular rounds of the divisions, a young man who was two or three tiers down the leadership ladder would always make a point of catching my attention.

'Give me a chance,' he'd say. 'If you give me a chance, I can show you what I can do.'

One day, there was an opening for a new general manager of his company. I thought long and hard about who to appoint to take over. Should I move someone over from one of our other companies? It would be the obvious choice to appoint a manager who had been successful elsewhere and had the experience to take the reins at this company. Or should I give this keen young man a chance? He had, after all, worked in the business for eight years, so most likely knew first-hand what the management dynamics were.

I decided to take a chance.

Even I was surprised by how rapidly he settled into the position, and the extent to which he improved overall performance. He had clearly been waiting for this moment, leaping into action immediately and tackling several challenges at once. In addition to making many of the sensible changes the company had needed, he also made great efforts towards motivating and re-energising the team, reminding them that they were integral to the rest of the business.

There were many things that happened here. Obviously, I empowered him to make those changes because I believed he could be successful, but he shone in his new role because he was hungry for the opportunity and had a different outlook from those who had been there before him. He questioned everything. All the years he had been waiting for the chance to make his mark, he had been carefully watching what was happening and making his own judgements about what he could do to improve the company's performance. He got to know the detail behind the business and was prepared to ask the tough questions. That made all the difference.

Natural leaders like this are the exception, but there are people like this in nearly all organisations. There is a balance, though. While leaders should always be on the lookout for potential stars who should be given a chance, there should always be a structured pipeline, training and developing individuals so they can rise from one tier to the next.

Tier Three: Managing managers to functional managers

Communication skills come to the fore here. At this stage, an individual becomes part of the business team, reporting to a business manager above them. Many of their previous peers will now report to them and they may be required to lead down at least two tiers. They could even be put in charge of areas of the business that they are unfamiliar with. At the same time, as functional managers, they may need to coordinate with others at the same level, meaning they need to become skilled at understanding issues across the organisation and the overall strategy everyone is working towards. There may be a sense of competition amongst departments for resources and more time will be spent in company-wide meetings. This is where individuals develop a longer-term perspective, alongside an increased awareness of changes to the overall market and the strategies of competitors.

Tier Four: Functional managers to business managers

While there are more new and unfamiliar responsibilities at this level than in possibly any of the other tiers, many business managers also cite this stage of their leadership journey as one of the most rewarding. This is the point where an individual acquires considerable autonomy in their role, making more of their own decisions and being held responsible for them. Equally importantly, they are more connected with the financial impact of their decision-making, with quarterly profit, market share, product and people targets. In planning any future activity, people in this position must consider the bottom line from both a short-term and a long-term perspective.

Tier Five: Business managers to group managers

This step up might, at first glance at least, seem quite straightforward. Managing a group of businesses is not that much more challenging than focusing on just one, or so the thinking might go. And there are, indeed, many complementary skills. However, a business manager is focused on just their own division of a company, whereas a group manager needs to see the bigger picture because they oversee several businesses.

A leader at this level needs to have both an internal and an external perspective. They are fully accountable and answerable to shareholders and also need to be able to think in broad terms to factor in the impact of external factors such as looming legislation, or changes in the competitive landscape.

Tier Six: Group managers to enterprise managers

The final tier is reserved for the top job, CEO or managing director. The focus of this position is centred more around values than skills. This is where the culture of the company is modelled, and the direction of travel for the business is set. The person at the top is ultimately responsible for the bottom line and must drive performance month by month, quarter by quarter. While still very much responsible for strategy, there is a shift towards visionary, outside-of-the-box thinking. Although there will be concern for individual parts of the business, the key focus will be on the performance of the whole company.

Each of these tiers comes with its own challenges. It is up to the overall leader to model the way and to help team members through each one, so that they develop their own leadership skills. Training is essential, as is providing assignments that stretch people so they can practise the necessary skills for the next level. We also run a mentoring programme, using both internal and external mentors to help our future leaders. When you invest in people, it builds their confidence, which in turn will make them surer of themselves. When people are sure of themselves, they produce better work.

Not everyone will be suitable for progression to each successive level. In fact, the number of people who move up will shrink significantly at each tier. Some natural leaders will rise to the top faster than others who may take their time to learn the necessary skills.

Experience has shown me that a natural leader invariably emerges in each of the tiers discussed here. They are easy to spot from the way they hold themselves or talk about any subject. When I look at them, I think to myself, *that is the one*. However, even then, it is essential that their progress is carefully managed. No one should be promoted before they are ready and have learned all the skills necessary to perform well in the next tier. Effective leadership results from perfecting a series of diverse skills over time. In the following chapter, I discuss succession planning for the top roles in a business, but in reality, a cut-down version of this process should be implemented for each tier. The appropriate requirements to move up to the next level should be defined, with a clearly laid-out selection process. If there are any gaps in training and experience, they should be addressed before someone is promoted.

Increasing the effectiveness of leaders

The team that inhabits the top few tiers of any organisation plays two critical roles. The first is quite obvious: to contribute to and carry out the strategy that will grow the business. This means using their expertise and skills in their particular department or division to meet goals they have helped set and produce consistent results. The second is less obvious but just as important, which is why I would like to highlight it here. This second role is to preserve the values of a business and ensure that everything that is done aligns with them. I view the senior team as ambassadors for the company, who see to it that the qualities of listening, empathy and kindness, respect, commitment, harmony and enthusiasm permeate every corner of the business. It is impossible to do this without them, because these behaviours permeate down from the top.

It is, of course, the responsibility of the overall leader to build and develop their team, and a crucial part of that begins with making sure that everyone properly understands and respects the company values. An effective leader is responsible for teaching, motivating and inspiring the senior team so that they understand the behaviour they need to model. After that, a leader needs to create an environment that will bring out the best in people, building on their individual strengths and weaknesses, as well as providing the resources to help them achieve great outcomes.

What every leader needs to realise is that not everyone will perform as expected or fully embrace the values of a business. However careful we are in the interview process, or at managing the promotion through each tier, it is not a given that even the highest performers will excel on every team and lead according to the values laid out. (The opposite is true too. Candidates that might not look impressive on paper can shine in the right environment.) The mismatch may not be immediately evident, but the team will soon spot someone who does not fully buy into the strategic purpose of a business. I want to work with people who have empathy and properly understand and respect my values.

11

Managing Change and Setting a Strategy for the Future

Innovation in business needs management.

My granddaughter told me about an interesting conversation that occurred shortly after my first book, a biography, was released. She'd been at school and a teacher had approached her to speak about the book and asked if the author was indeed her grandmother.

'Can you ask her a question for me?' he asked. 'In the picture on the front cover, she is standing and looking outside the window. Why doesn't she look ahead? It makes for a nicer picture when you make eye contact with the reader.'

When this exchange was relayed to me, I was amused.

'Please tell him that your grandmother said that she's looking at the horizon to see what she can find there,' I told her. 'I'm already thinking of many new things that I can achieve. There is a whole world to look at.'

This is my philosophy. I am always looking to see what else I can do and how I can make my business more successful. This is how to protect its soul, now and in the future. Many on my leadership team think the same way. We often ask ourselves: what can we do to grow this business?

The burning ambition to constantly grow and improve is a guiding principle we share with the UAE, the country that has been home for the Easa Saleh Al Gurg Group since the company first opened for business in Dubai in 1960. In fact, we have always viewed our growth in parallel. The leaders of the UAE have for some years pursued a far-sighted vision for this country's place in the world. Between 2000 and 2019, the UAE's GDP quadrupled in current terms, boasting a 41 per cent share of foreign direct investment projects that have been attracted to Arab countries between 2003 and 2021.

In recent times, those plans have accelerated, with the UAE introducing sweeping reforms to drive social, legal and economic liberalisation and attract even more foreign investment. The mega-exhibition, Expo 2020 Dubai, which attracted 25 million visitors, showcased innovation from a vast number of home-grown businesses. We saw everything from 'energy trees', to the world's largest projection screen, to countless robots. Meanwhile, there are a long list of growth initiatives included in other projects, such as the Dubai 2040 Master Plan, with its goal of sustainable urban development, as well as the global entrepreneurship programme Scale2Dubai. It all adds up to the fact that the UAE is a very exciting place to do business right now.

All of this does, however, need to be weighed against the global trading environment we are in. At the time of writing, the world is entering an uncertain economic period in the aftermath of the pandemic. Inflation is rising, many businesses are scaling back, and there has been a contraction in consumer spending.

While it is not always possible to predict the future, particularly when so many events in the world are moving at such a pace, we can pursue strategies that both maintain growth and set us up to continue in this way. In the following sections, I share some thoughts on how to do this.

Diversify

There are many businesses that have succeeded with just one great product for a mass audience. The idea is that it keeps things simple because customers know exactly what they are getting and, since the brand is entirely focused on one product, it has to be good. This may well be the case, and certainly so with well-known brands. However, in a time of low growth, or in a very competitive market, it can be challenging when you only have one product to rely on.

In a tough market, a diversified trading strategy removes a lot of uncertainty because products and services can be sold across a range of different markets. Certainly, the diversification of our business has stood us in good stead through a series of challenging circumstances in the past, such as the Gulf War, Iraq War and fluctuations in the economy, such as the Global Financial Crisis in 2008.

Managing a diversified conglomerate opens up a world of opportunities. When we go into a tendering process, for example, our consultants have the pick of a range of products and materials from within our company. Capitalising on every asset you own is the way to build a business. For this to succeed, you need to be totally immersed in the ins and outs of the business and know exactly what each division can produce within what timescale.

Not everything a business ventures into works. That is the nature of ambitious leadership. Occasionally, we will try one thing and it will develop in a different way than we expected. Similarly, we will enter into new partnerships and not all of them will be successful. The important thing is that we are on top of each solution, and properly investigate each one to make informed decisions.

Identify and manage risk

I have never feared change. Things change all the time, and either you move with them and grow, or you stand still and get left behind. Businesses should always be aware of risks, or potential pitfalls in the future. These risks can emerge from a variety of sources, be it changes in legislation or business processes, developments in technology or the emergence of a competitive threat. All leaders should be knowledgeable about world issues and adopt broad thinking practices, so they are fully prepared to adapt to any major change. They should be constantly asking themselves how these developments will impact their business. It is crucial to address any risks well ahead of time.

Leaders should be learning all the time. It is imperative that we are aware of political and economic developments in our region and others where we trade. It is only when we are fully armed with the latest knowledge that we can adapt to these changes. Everyone in the business is encouraged to think in this way, and the senior leadership team do not keep their findings to themselves. When we see a change is coming, an analysis is shared widely in every area of the organisation, so everyone can contribute ideas on the best way forward. We have regular discussions on how to improve and shape the business for the future.

Leadership is not only about you but about all your surroundings

Listen to customers and observe their behaviour

While running a business, it is easy to get swept away by developing and selling products without pausing to think about who is buying them, how and why. This would be a huge mistake for any consumer-facing business today. One of the most significant changes we have observed in the evolution of our business has occurred over the past decade. Modern customers are entirely different. They gravitate to online shopping and, even if they travel to a physical location to buy their goods, they are highly informed. They have all the information they need about the products they want to buy at their fingertips. And they expect immediate turnaround.

The success of any organisation is based on keeping customer requirements at the core of how day-to-day business is conducted. To do this, businesses need to:

○ Listen *and* observe. Customers can sometimes be poor at communicating exactly what they want, so observing their behaviour and what they actually buy is just as important.

○ Follow trends. Tastes change, as do customer perceptions of the value of a product. Businesses need to embrace this and, where possible, anticipate change.

○ Respond quickly to any feedback, questions and, in particular, complaints.

○ Use customer insight tools. There are plenty of tools that show what customers are talking about online: use them to track what they are saying about your business. Respond and participate in discussions where appropriate.

Deploy a digital transformation strategy

Digital transformation is the cornerstone of any strategy to future-proof business. We all recognise that the internet is essential to customer experience and engagement, thanks to the increased demand for e-commerce. However, this is not the only area where businesses can maximise their potential. Technology is an essential part of operational efficiency, and all companies should have a full digital transformation strategy that examines every aspect of their portfolio to see how digitalisation can simplify and speed up processes and make them more efficient.

We have regular conversations about our digital transformation strategy because the digital world moves so quickly. We consider it from every angle, from what new developments are on the horizon to what our competitors are doing. We constantly ask ourselves, *What can we do next? How can we become more efficient?*

Predict future demand, today

All businesses want to stay one step ahead of competitors, which is a challenge in a fast-moving world, where information travels faster than ever. You need a laser-focused understanding of your customers because they won't always tell you what they want. Businesses need to be able to predict consumers' future demands before the consumers themselves even realise them.

What was good 10 years ago
may not be relevant today

The key to getting this right is to understand the industries you work in and to keep a close eye on trends. Once again, technology is your friend here, as there is a large amount of data that gives great insights into customer behaviour. Also, remember that your own sales team will have first-hand news of what people are saying and what is catching their eye. This is where an efficient in-house communication system can pay dividends in identifying and passing on patterns of behaviour. Plus, while it might sound counter-intuitive, it can be useful to look to the past to make predictions for the future.

We know that, for example, in economic downturns, consumers will rein in spending. This has implications for every area of our operations.

Changes in consumer behaviour don't usually happen overnight. Rather, they come gradually and in a systematic way, often over several years. However, the time to prepare for these changes is now.

Once a leader understands upcoming changes, they can create the necessary infrastructure to support them. Ensuring a business is future-proof is a key role for any leader.

Ensure growth is stable and sustainable

Our strategy today is, as it always has been, to grow the business. Moving forward, we endeavour to do so in a more sustainable way. It will never be a case of growth at all costs. We want steady, manageable, long-term growth because we are here for the long haul. Therefore, as documented here, we are constantly evaluating where the business is now, what works and what doesn't, and setting measurable goals for the future.

There will always be competition. We are, for example, seeing an increasing number of new players in our markets. Thanks to technology, the barriers to entry are smaller than at any time previously, and we find ourselves competing with businesses with lower overheads than ours when we go out to tender for large projects. This does not, however, mean we will take unreasonable risks to win business, or cut corners just to maintain momentum. Our reputation as a business is precious, and so is our name. We fully understand that our continued growth is very much tied in with customer satisfaction. Our clients and partners stay with us because they know they can trust us.

More so than anything else, our authenticity and our values contribute to our business's stability, protecting and strengthening its soul and purpose. While we are rightly proud of our strategy, processes and systems, it is the human qualities we offer that sustain our growth. Everything we do is aligned to our culture of listening, empathy, kindness, trust and respect. These values have always been the filter through which we make all our important business decisions. Our values are not just there for show. They are the foundation for our growth.

12

Business Continuity and Succession Planning

Money flows, but legacy remains.

When I first joined the Easa Saleh Al Gurg Group, I wanted to learn everything. My brain was like a sponge, soaking up every aspect of the business. I would go to every meeting with a notebook and write pages and pages of notes, which I would go through later in the day to make sure I had not missed a thing. One day, I was sitting in a meeting, scribbling away in my notebook, when there was a brief pause in conversation. I looked up from my notes and saw that the Chairman was staring at me. The silence in the room seemed to grow between us and I was tempted to look down at my notebook to see if I had missed something. Yet I could not tear myself away from his gaze. Then, he raised his hand and said one word.

'Listen,' he said.

His message was succinct, but clear. If I wanted to become a good leader, I needed to put down my pen and really listen. It was useful to take notes, but my energies would be much better spent engaging with what was being said in real time. This is how I would understand and appreciate the soul of this business, which I would one day be charged with passing on to the next generation.

This was just one of hundreds of lessons passed on to me by the Chairman. He began this process the moment I started in the business because he was fully focused on the issue of succession, even though it was decades before he was due to retire. He understood that there is nothing more vital to a company's long-term health than the choice and cultivation of the leaders who will protect its soul and take it to the next stage of growth. To achieve a smooth, effortless transition, there needs to be careful planning and evaluation.

The Easa Saleh Al Gurg Group is a family business, but the lessons in this final chapter are crucial for any business, large or small, in public or private hands. As previously detailed, ensuring the pipeline is filled with a good supply of high-performing people is a key priority of any leader. Then, if one person leaves the organisation, another talented individual is there to take their place. No time is wasted on a lengthy recruitment process, or waiting for them to learn about the job. They are up and ready straight away. The most important part of this pipeline is for the leadership of the organisation as a whole. Safeguarding the continuity and continued growth of the business is one of the most important roles of any leader.

Share knowledge and information.
Others will value your leadership more

There is so much more to succession planning than identifying a list of candidates to take over when the incumbent leader retires or moves on. As the Chairman correctly identified, it is closely tied in with the process of leadership development.

Too many businesses fail to think about the second line, or plan succession for critical roles. They are too focused on the here and now. Why is it that some leaders are so cautious about creating concrete succession plans and developing the next layer of talent? Perhaps they have a subconscious aversion to the suggestion that they won't be around forever. Or they are too caught up with the challenges of the day to plan for the future. I suspect it may also come down to insecurity. Leaders may worry that if they bring in someone beneath them, the new person may do a better job, or the team may respond to them more positively, and somehow, it will undermine their position. Also, they may be counselled by others on the board who are concerned that starting the process could be perceived as a lack of confidence in the current leadership team and destabilise the organisation.

By its nature, if done properly, succession planning can take many years to bear fruit. Most companies, particularly those in the public domain, have narrower time horizons. With shareholders to answer to, their focus tends to be on the next quarter or, at a stretch, on the next year. The only time the word 'succession' is mentioned in the boardroom is just before the CEO or chairman is about to leave.

Perhaps, though, the biggest reason why this crucial aspect of leadership is frequently neglected is there is no clear process in place. Nearly all businesses have clear methodology for financial oversight, or project planning, or compensation, but somehow succession is not on the radar. No one owns the problem. There is no clarity about whether this is the responsibility of the chairman, the CEO, the whole board or HR. When no one is ultimately accountable, it is easy for succession to slip down the list of priorities.

What everyone needs to realise is that leadership is not a right. The post is not ours come what may. In business, however, things can change in a moment, and we need to prepare for every eventuality. It is the duty of all businesses to be proactive and disciplined about this process. There are multiple benefits to succession planning that go beyond mere business continuity.

Planning for succession well ahead of time protects a business from any sudden and unexpected change. While every aspect of company growth is important to me, it would be illogical for me to become too swept up in the day-to-day issues impacting our business to the exclusion of all other considerations. My goal is to pass on a successful company with bright prospects for its future. I have no idea how long I will be here, or even how long it will be practical for me to remain active in the company. Succession plans are, therefore, part of our overall growth strategy.

Earlier, I wrote about the strategic plan that we have written for the next three years and explained that we are already working towards writing the next one. The issue of succession is very much tied into this plan, because the issue of succession is a multidisciplinary process. To properly plan for the future there needs to be a deep understanding of the present and where the opportunities lie. The development of new leadership and the structures put in place to support them is not something we can leave until the last minute. If we did, it would be chaos, and chaos is hugely destructive for any business. Not only would it leave everyone within the business deeply unsettled, but it would also allow competitors to point the finger.

We are already realising another key benefit of planning succession well in advance: an injection of some highly innovative talent. What is most important is that each person on the senior team has brought with them some remarkable skills, which are already helping the business grow and thrive in a wide range of areas. Again, any business planning for its future will encounter the same benefits. By bringing in the next generation of leaders in good time, it will immediately have an impact. Ambitious and talented executives can help identify any weaknesses in processes, uncover new sales opportunities and markets, and other, as yet unrealised potential in the business. It also encourages companies to formalise their processes for training and professional development to prepare executives to step up when the time comes. By this, I mean more than training courses and learning materials. We need to offer opportunities for coaching, mentoring and job shadowing.

In this final chapter, I would like to go through my rules for smooth succession. They are based on what I have learned about the process from a family business viewpoint, but I believe they are relevant for any business.

Focus on planning and development

The first rule of creating a succession plan is to get on with it. Succession planning is, or at least should be, an important and evolving process. It can take years of refinement to properly set the stage for the next generation of leadership and can't be put off until some vague time in the future. It should be introduced as part of a business's strategy and operations at the earliest opportunity.

The goal of my own succession plan is to pass the business over as smoothly as it was handed over to me. I have not restricted my thinking to simply working out who will replace me. While some businesses think of succession planning as a high-level exercise (if they consider it at all), concentrating their efforts on finding a new CEO, my approach was to look across the whole business, from the leadership team to the divisional heads. One of my first acts upon taking over in our business was to create a committee to scrutinise future roles across the company. I did not put myself at the top of this committee; I invited another senior member of my leadership team to head up this endeavour. Their leadership style and personal values will inevitably be different from my own, but it is to all our benefits to take diverse views into consideration from the beginning and to base the future strategy for the business on this outlook.

Once the process has begun, the fundamental rule of succession planning is to focus on developing the next generation. It is not a question of bringing people in just to fill a slot. Succession planning needs to be closely linked to leadership development, to help each new leader develop the skills they need.

When new team members join the company, whether family or otherwise, we think carefully about where they are best suited. We are all unique, not only in our capabilities, but also in our capacity for growth and development and the interests we want to pursue. Building a succession strategy involves a lot of listening. The head of the company needs to listen to others and understand their viewpoint and visions for the future. It might be that everyone has a different idea on future direction. In fact, it is highly possible. The goal is to find a direction that everyone can agree on, which may involve a combination of people's views. What is important is that this process is given time to develop.

It is crucial to understand where each individual executive's best talents lie. Some future leaders may be curious and insightful and therefore more orientated towards strategic planning and key projects. Others might be good at engaging and inspiring other people and will therefore be better at team and change leadership. These are assessments that need to be made when assigning people to the appropriate division or department, based on their interests and abilities.

Just to add to the complication of the forward planning process, there is not a one-to-one correlation between leadership competencies present in the organisation today versus the ones that might be needed tomorrow. When my sisters joined the business, it was a very different one from the one it is today.

When reviewing succession, we can't think in terms of an organisational chart, replacing a person in one role with a younger version of themselves with similar skills. Like I say, our business has changed. This means that, when planning the next generation of leadership, thought must be given to the functions needed today and in the future. Again, this was something we looked at in our planning process, asking ourselves a number of questions, such as, *How will our product mix, customer base and supply chain change? What roles do we need in place to service the company we are driving towards becoming? What type of person will these roles demand?*

When determining the best fit for future roles we are careful to think about the process from all angles. We are defining what we want from our future generation of leaders based on our future strategy and ambitions for results, and then matching them according to their abilities, entrepreneurial talent and commitment to our values. But what are we offering in return? The next generation of leaders are highly skilled, which was why we identified them as the right fit. However, they could easily be richly rewarded elsewhere. Like any business, we need to offer our future leaders an opportunity they simply wouldn't get with another company. Competitive compensation is not enough to retain leaders with the best potential. They also seek opportunities to make an impact and grow their abilities, as well as the freedom to work alongside existing leadership to create ambitious plans for the future. We need to both respect and encourage this.

A significant part of what we offer is learning and development, which is something we have found to be of value to the new generation of leaders. As well as structured leadership development training, we also provide the opportunity for them to gain experience across different functions and lead special project and innovation teams. This is very much the strategy I followed when I joined the business, working in each division for several months before moving to the next one.

Creating learning and development opportunities is a priority, but so is passing on my own knowledge. Succession in a business is about so much more than simply handing on ownership. It is also the process of handing over the knowledge, relationships and authority that have been carefully built up in a business over the years. I make a point of speaking with my senior team on a daily basis, both formally in meetings and informally over a quick cup of morning coffee. I also speak with the more junior members, every two or three weeks as a matter of course. They are encouraged to come and speak with me whenever they like if there is anything pressing, just like the rest of the team.

Be transparent

Giving yourself time to prepare facilitates a sequential approach, where responsibilities are gradually awarded to the new generation, so that they have ample time to adapt. The goal here is that the next generation doesn't see itself as living in the shadow of the current leadership, but rather steadily building autonomy with their new responsibilities and duties. This is far more productive than a situation where the business leader wields unquestioned authority, holding on to all the most important tasks. This would result in an environment in which the next generation of leaders are unprepared to take on complex tasks.

I have been open about discussing the business in front of my family, even from a young age. Some of my earliest memories involve listening to my father take calls from business partners around the world. In the beginning, I had no idea what he was talking about. I'd be conscious that he'd be talking to a business in, say, Switzerland, and wonder how he'd become involved with this company. Listening to him taught me so much. I followed the same strategy with the next generation. I will always speak openly about business in front of them. It is part of the learning experience.

While developing the right range of skills to ensure consistent results is key, it is equally important to protect the values which have built and shaped the business. Every leader will, of course, wish to put their own stamp on the business when the time comes, but there are ways to ensure this is from the position of understanding the core brand and what it means to customers and employees.

As with so many aspects of leadership, there is a balance to be had. Senior leaders should be wary of being too rigid and prescriptive. Setting all the rules and maintaining a single-minded focus will deny the next generation the experience they need to understand and develop their own values. It is far better to create an environment of open communication and transparency about shared values and norms, inviting discussion and debate about future direction.

In the past, the Chairman would discuss with me what he felt worked and didn't work within the business. I have followed the same style. If I don't like a course of action, then I will speak up with respect and consideration. However, while I make my views clear because I pride myself on being transparent and on having nothing to hide, I accept there is always an alternative viewpoint. I am perfectly happy to hear other points of view.

One of my main objectives in planning succession is to make sure my team is completely ready for whatever comes next. This means I have made a conscious effort to step aside, to empower them to develop in their roles and take responsibility for their decisions.

Sometimes space is better than interference

Whatever level in the firm the prospective leadership team reaches, I urge everyone to take full responsibility in their roles. Whenever a decision is made, I make sure everyone signs off on it so there is collective accountability. Again, this is a crucial part of the transition process.

Challenges specific to family business succession

While we have the infrastructure of any large corporation, we are still at heart a family business. We need to accept that there are challenges and an added layer of complexity that will always be unique to our type of businesses, since the fortunes of the company and the unity of the family are both at stake. Since this is an area where I have extensive experience, I have included this section since it might be of interest for anyone running their own family business who is considering the best way to pass the baton to the next generation.

The first challenge is one of perception. Every family member who joins the business should be aware that they will inevitably be judged to a higher standard than anyone else on the team. To maintain team morale across all departments and divisions, it is crucial that there is no favouritism or special treatment. No one should use their name to overstep their authority or take any actions that undermine anyone else on the senior team.

I have made it clear to each member of the family who joins us that my expectations are high. If anything, I expect them to meet considerably higher standards than anyone else in the organisation, because I want to be transparent.

It is for this reason that every family member who has ever joined our business has always had a job elsewhere beforehand. The Chairman felt strongly that this was important, so everyone gains life experience and builds upon their skill base. I completely agree with this philosophy and know how much I learned, and indeed brought with me, from my previous career leading a school. When someone has had extensive external experience, it means that when they start at the company, they are ready to make a meaningful contribution. They will have already developed people skills and built relationships that may be useful in the future, and they will arrive ready to contribute in a professional manner. Everyone in our business needs to add value.

Communication is a significant issue in a family business because the company is generally the prime source of the family's income and wealth – past and future. Therefore, each family member will have a vested interest in the progress of the business and the plans and decisions being made. They will also expect to have a voice.

It is in all our interests to think carefully about the future. It is not simply because it is the legacy of the Chairman, of whom we are rightly proud. It is a legacy that the whole family has played a part in creating. That is a legacy well worth protecting.

Afterword

What do I see for the future of the Easa Saleh Al Gurg Group? We are close to reaching a time when that will be very much for the next generation to decide. During my many years leading this business, we have introduced many new processes to chart a course for the coming years, but the way in which these will be interpreted won't be up to me. I am, however, confident that the business my father founded is in very good hands and the third generation will do the right thing for the family as a whole. I am positive the business will continue to grow as an international force to be reckoned with, as we explore new opportunities in new regions.

It is highly likely the dynamic will continue to change. That is the nature of progress. During the first generation of a business like ours, the focus is always on the person who created the business, in this case my father and the powerful legacy he created. By the time the third generation takes over, it is inevitable that the focus switches to the business itself. This will be especially so with the Easa Saleh Al Gurg Group, since it spans across so many divisions and has so many areas of growth.

As for the second generation, and my contribution, I will let you be the judge of my effectiveness as a leader. I like to think that I have been true to the style of authentic leadership I aspire to. When it comes to the *mind* part of the authenticity, I am still as interested and enthusiastic about the business as I ever have been, perhaps even more so with each passing year.

My role has changed a lot since the early days of becoming a managing director. The business has grown considerably and trades across many regions and sectors. I still make an effort to visit the various divisions often. It is not as often as it was in the beginning, because I have many other commitments, but I do like to make my presence known. I still interact with staff at all levels, to listen to their views, because this is where the real innovation comes from. I am constantly inspired by so many of the initiatives the team have pursued, and I take time to learn about each new development to properly understand how it fits into the bigger picture. I still read as much as I ever did and make sure to go through the minutes of all the company meetings, even if I am unable to attend. It makes me smile when a member of the senior team will drop by my office to update me on a project and I will already know everything they are telling me.

'How do you know about this?' they will say, in surprise. 'You've been away from the office on business for a week.'

I remind them that I like to know everything about the company that bears my family name and will always take the time to find out what is happening. Even when I am on holiday, I am never really on holiday. I still read my daily reports with great interest.

Equally important is the *heart* of authentic leadership. The values I hold closest to me have done much to shape the business as it is now, and I am proud of that. If you were to replace the question that opened this afterword with *What would I like to see for the future of the Easa Saleh Al Gurg Group?* I would answer that it is important to me that these values are maintained, so the people within the business continue to trust, respect and help one another. I would like to think that everyone's contribution will always be listened to, and everyone will feel emboldened to speak from the heart. This is crucial to maintain the culture of innovation which has long been the foundation of our growth. Similarly, I will feel I have done a good job if the present and future team still prioritise empathy and kindness. Together, these qualities will maintain the enthusiasm everyone holds for what this business can yet do. When we are happy and excited about our work, success is never far behind.

As for the *soul* of the business, I believe it is clear from the final three chapters how important creating the legacy of this business is to me. Everything we have done is done with one eye on securing the company for years to come, whether it is in the strength of our plans and processes or the diverse skills of our leadership teams.

My own personal sense of relevance is not dependent on the family business, even though I am deeply attached to it. I have always had an interest in many other areas too. I will be quite happy to transition my knowledge and energy into these interests. I see myself increasing my philanthropy work, both for my father's charity and other foundations.

The business has also led to many important and lasting connections and relationships, which will continue to be part of my life. Through the Dubai Business Women Council, I am, for example, involved in its mentorship programme. This highly inspirational programme, which is in its fourth year, is taking great strides towards the personal and professional development of women in the UAE by challenging bias and creating opportunities. It has already helped train and mentor more than 100 entrepreneurs in areas as diverse as banking and financial services, real estate, fashion and beauty, and technology. As I said at the start of this book, the message of empowering women in leadership roles is one I have always been in great favour of, and I would certainly want to do more to help other women leaders. It is in all our interests to create an even playing field so more women get the opportunity to shine in business. Women are just as equipped as men to be truly authentic leaders and, arguably, could be said to be more naturally prone to displaying some of the qualities that define this sort of leadership. The authentic leadership style does, after all, flourish in people who are genuine, self-aware and transparent, as it requires us to show who we are as a person. This is what inspires trust and loyalty among teams. These are all qualities that seem to come quite easily to women.

My advice to any leader, male or female, is to forget about trying to be an assertive, or confident, or inspirational leader. Think instead about being you. Authentic leadership comes from realising your own potential. What are the qualities that mean the most to you? What moves you? Build your leadership style around these values and share them with your team every day. Dedicate yourself to learning. A lot. All the time. Whatever you do, find out everything you can about the subject in which your business specialises. When you talk about your business and what it does, you should always be the most knowledgeable person in the room. Not that you should be talking all the time. Listening more than talking is always far more productive. Finally, think about the future. What is it you want your legacy to be? Work towards building a business and a team that will last far into the future.

I wish you good fortune with your own leadership and in your own business.

Appendix

Recommended reading

My deep and lasting thirst for knowledge has led me to read a large number of leadership books, among other works of non-fiction. I am sharing here some of the titles I have found most useful.

Building a Successful Family Business Board: A guide for leaders, directors and families – Jennifer M. Pendergast, John L. Ward, Stephanie Brun De Pontet (Palgrave Macmillan – 8 March 2011)

Business Made Simple: 60 days to master leadership, sales, marketing, execution, management, personal productivity and more – Donald Miller (HarperCollins Leadership – 19 January 2021)

The Coaching Habit: Say less, ask more, and change the way you lead forever – Bungay Stanier (Page Two – 29 February 2016)

Conscious Leadership: Elevating humanity through business – John Mackey, Steve McIntosh, Carter Phipps (Bantam Press – 17 September 2020)

Dare to Lead: Brave work, tough conversations, whole hearts – Brené Brown (Random House – 9 October 2018)

Energy Leadership: Transforming your workplace and your life from the core, the 7 level framework for mastery in life and business – Bruce D. Schneider (Wiley – 11 Aug 2022)

Family Business Succession: The final test of greatness – C. Aronoff, S. McClure, J. Ward (Palgrave Macmillan – 11 Jan 2011)

Honest to Greatness: How today's greatest leaders use brutal honesty to achieve success – Peter Kozodoy (BenBella Books – 11 August 2020)

How Successful People Lead: Taking your influence to the next level – John C. Maxwell (Center Street – 21 May 2013)

How to Win Friends and Influence People – Dale Carnegie (Vermillion – 6 April 2006)

Keeping the Family Business Healthy: How to plan for continuing growth, profitability, and family leadership – John L. Ward (Palgrave MacMillan – 11 January 2011)

Lean in: Women, work, and the will to lead – Sheryl Sandberg (Knopf Doubleday Publishing Group – 11 March 2013)

Leaders Eat Last: Why some teams pull together and others don't – Simon Sinek (Portfolio – 25 May 2017)

Leading in a Culture of Change – Michael Fullan (Jossey-Bass – (10 February 2020)

Lincoln on Leadership: Executive strategies for tough times – Donald T. Phillips (Little Brown US – 12 March 1998)

Start With Why: How great leaders inspire everyone to take action – Simon Sinek (Portfolio – 1 January 2009)

The Art of Negotiation: How to improve agreement in a chaotic world – Michael Wheeler (Simon & Schuster – 8 October 2013)

The Art of Thinking Clearly: Better thinking, better decisions – Rolf Dobelli (Sceptre – 8 May 2014)

The Family Council Handbook: How to create, run and maintain a successful family business council – Christopher J. Eckrich, Stephen L. McClure (Palgrave Macmillan – 16 July 2012)

The Leader in You: How to win friends, influence people and succeed in a changing world – Dale Carnegie (Pocket Books – 1993)

The Leader Who Had No Title: A modern fable on real success in business and in life – Robin Sharma (Free Press – 23 March 2010)

The Leadership Challenge: How to make extraordinary things happen in organisations – James M. Kouzes, Barry Z. Posner (Jossey-Bass – 13 June 2017)

The Leadership Pipeline: How to build the leadership powered company – Stephen Drotter, Ram Charan, James L. Noel (Jossey-Bass – 28 January 2011)

The Leadership Skills Handbook: 100 essential skills you need to be a leader – Jo Owen (Kogan Page – 3rd October 2020)

The Making of Leader: What elite sport can teach us about leadership, management and performance – Tom Young (Robinson – 30 July 2020)

The Making of a Manager: What to do when everyone looks to you – Julie Zhuo (Virgin Books – 21 March 2019)

The Mind of the Leader: How to lead yourself, your people, and your organisation for extraordinary results – Rasmus Hougaard, Jacqueline Carter (Harvard Business Review Press – 13 March 2018)

The Nine Types of Leader: How the leaders of tomorrow can learn from the leaders of today – James Ashton (Kogan Page – 3 January 2021)

The Power of Leadership – John C. Maxwell (Honor Books – 20 January 2001)

The Truth about Leaderships: The no-fads, heart of the matter facts you need to know – James M. Kouzes, Barry Z. Posner (Jossey-Bass – 17 September 2010)

Thinking, Fast and Slow – Daniel Kahneman (Penguin – 10 May 2012)

The Rules of Wealth: A personal code for prosperity and plenty – Richard Templar (Pearson – 6 August 2015)

Top Ten Mistakes Leaders Make – Dr Hans Finzel (CreateSpace Independent Publishing Platform – 21 February 2017)

The 21 Irrefutable Laws of Leadership: Follow them and people will follow you – John C. Maxwell (Thomas Nelson – 1 September 2007)

Women and Leadership: Lessons from some of the world's most powerful women – Julia Gillard (Corgi – 3 June 2021)

7 Paths to Managerial Leadership: Doing well by doing it right – Fred MacKenzie (ATD – 30 May 2016)

100 Things Successful People Do: Little exercise for successful living, 100 self help rules for life – Nigel Cumberland (John Murray Learning – 11 August 2016)